Athens disclosed

Denis Roubien

Copyright © 2021 Denis Roubien
All rights reserved
ISBN: 9798474496696

This book is dedicated to my long-standing co-hiker
in the discovery of Athens

Contents

1	A complicated city	1
2	Understanding modern Athens. The three grids	5
3	Frissiras Museum. The ancient monument that inspired a house	7
4	Monument of Lysicrates. The miniature library	9
5	A bourgeois dwelling of Ottoman times. The survival of ancient houses	13
6	A bourgeois dwelling after Independence. Neoclassical in the front, traditional in the back	15
7	A neoclassical facade in a pre-revolutionary house	17
8	Saint Nicholas Ragava. How to distinguish a Byzantine church	19
9	The last pre-revolutionary tower in Athens	23
10	The last mansion of pre-revolutionary Athens	25
11	Gorgoepikoos (small cathedral). A link between ancient times and the Middle Ages	27
12	Saints Anarghyri. Religious architecture after Byzantium	29
13	The house of the creator of modern Athens	30
14	The last bath of Ottoman times in Athens	32
15	The Roman Forum	34
16	The Madrasa	37
17	The Fethiye Mosque	39
18	The Library of Hadrian and the church on the stairs	41
19	The Tzistarakis Mosque	43
20	Monastiraki. The Great Monastery that became Small	45
21	Saint Eleousa: from a church to a courthouse	46
22	Academy of Athens. The exception on the list	49
23	The modern city of Athens. The 'monumental axis' and its relationship with the antiquities	50
24	The 'great promenade'. The connection of the archaeological sites of Athens with the modern city	65
	The Arch of Hadrian	67
	The temple of Zeus	69
	The ancient Stadium (Kallimarmaro)	70
	The northern and southern slopes of the Acropolis	71
	The Theatre of Dionysus	73
	The Asclepieion	74
	The Odeon of Herodes Atticus	74
	The Acropolis	76
	The Areopagus	85
	The archaeological site of Philopappou	86
	The Pnyx	86
	Transformation of the lower part of Hermes street into a pedestrian zone	87
	The ancient cemetery of the Kerameikos and Kerameikos square	89
	Transformation of Hadrian street into a pedestrian zone	93
	The Ancient Agora	94

Preface

This book's purpose is to help you understand what travel guides don't explain. You can find a lot of books on ancient Athens. If you get there, a guided tour will give you all the information you will need. But what about Athens in the centuries that followed? What about the old houses, old churches, mosques, and other obscure sights you stumble upon everywhere? This book, written by a specialist of Athens, apart from presenting all the major sights of Athens of all times, will help you understand the city of today and not feel lost as a visitor.

1. A complicated city

Apart from the traditional visit to the major archaeological sites of Athens, where you will probably read all the necessary information in your guidebooks or hear it from your guide, perhaps you will want to walk in the historical centre of Athens. And then you will see many things that no guide has explained to you. You will see houses like this.

And then, perhaps, next to it, something like this.

And, then again, farther down, something like this.

And even something like this.

Some centuries separate these buildings from one another. Centuries during which Athens, long after the end of the ancient world, passed from the Byzantine Empire to the Duchy of Athens, governed successively by the French, the Catalans, and the Florentines, and then to the Ottoman Empire, before becoming the capital of the new-born Greek state. Thus, the visitors will see, among the famous antiquities, many other buildings, which will make it difficult for them to understand this city of such a complex history.

The purpose of this book is to explain to you exactly that. Not by accumulating a lot of names and dates you will never be able to remember. But by using some characteristic examples, to make you understand the whole.

First, let us see how Athens was during centuries before it became the capital of Greece. It occupied almost the same area as in ancient times. The street network was always irregular, because of the ground's irregularity. In the following plan, you see the city with its major archaeological sites, although they had not been excavated yet and most of the antiquities were not visible. The walls were not those of ancient times but dated only from the 18th century. Nevertheless, their tracing often almost coincided with the ancient ones.

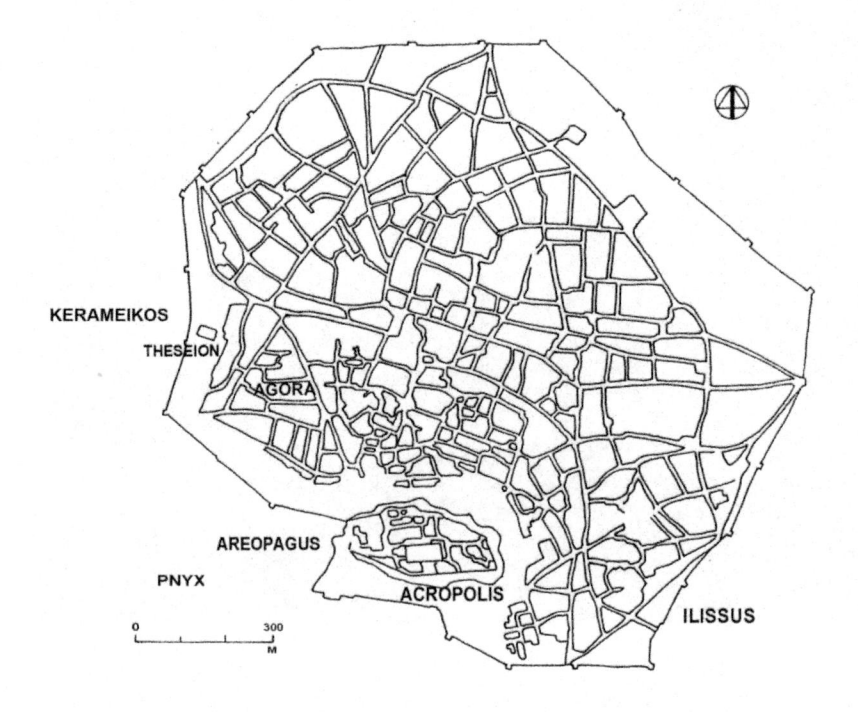

Athens before the Greek Independence (drawn by the author)

2. Understanding modern Athens. The three grids

When Athens became the capital of Greece in 1834, a modern city was added as an extension of the old one. But this time it was regular, as a modern European capital should be. The new city was formed according to three grids, arranged around a triangle that surrounded and at the same time penetrated the old town.

In this plan, you can easily distinguish the old town which was incorporated to the new one. It is the whole irregular part. And the stars are the twenty sights, mostly obscure, that this book proposes to you if you want to understand what you see, beyond the famous classical antiquities, which, of course, don't form the city's major part. The selected sights are within the area generally known as Plaka. The twentieth one is an exception, but in fact, it is just the link to another tour we will take later in the new city and its monuments.

The first part of this book will focus on the sights you will not find in any tourist guide, or if you do, for some, you will not have the crucial remarks that will help you understand the links between the city's different layers.

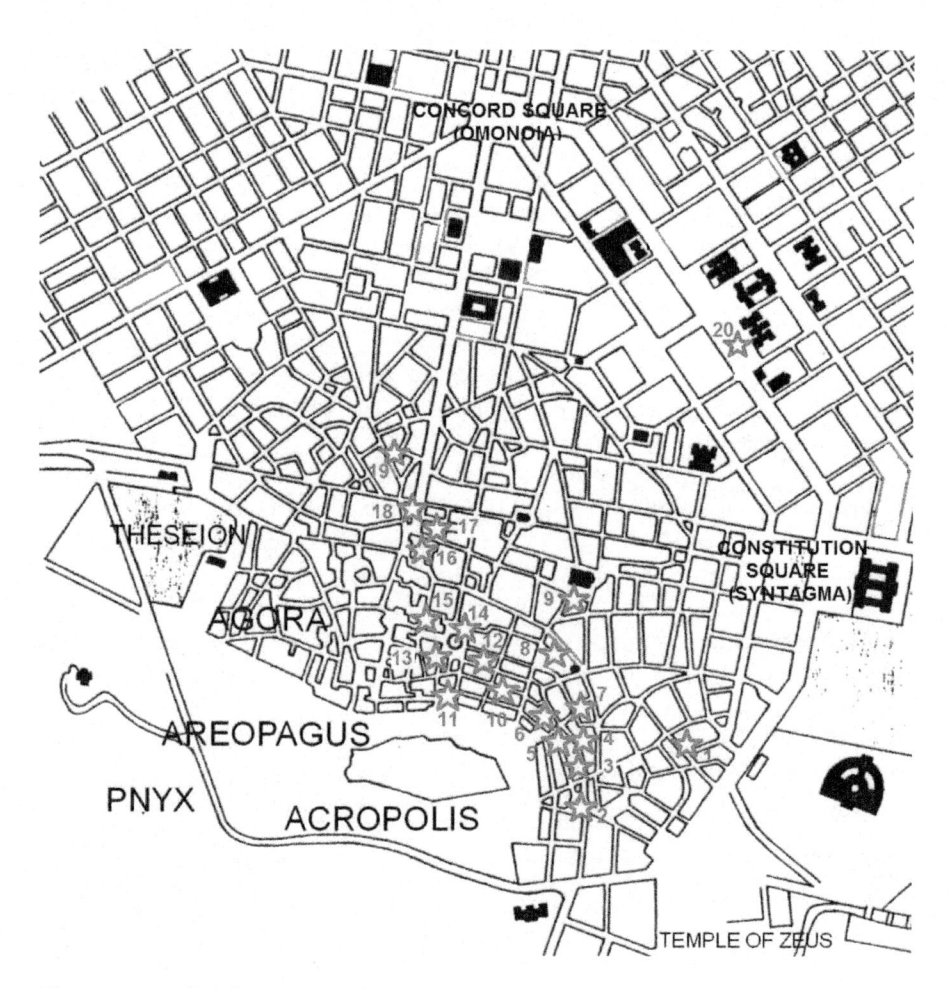

The centre of Athens with the sights included in this itinerary (drawn by the author)

3. Frissiras Museum
The ancient monument that inspired a house

Frissiras Museum

We start our tour with Frissiras Museum, in Monis Asteriou Street. It's a museum of contemporary European painting, housed in a building of the early 20th century, a work of Ernst Ziller. He was a German architect who spent most of his life in Greece and has signed hundreds of buildings. His name will appear many times if you occupy yourself at all with Greek neoclassical architecture.

But, apart from the museum's interest per se, this building is very characteristic of the wish of the Greeks after Independence to emulate the ancient monuments, in order to feel that they connected with their ancestors. Its rich appearance characterizes the late stages of classicism when the decorative elements became abundant.

If you wonder about the building's strange shape, let's move to the next sight.

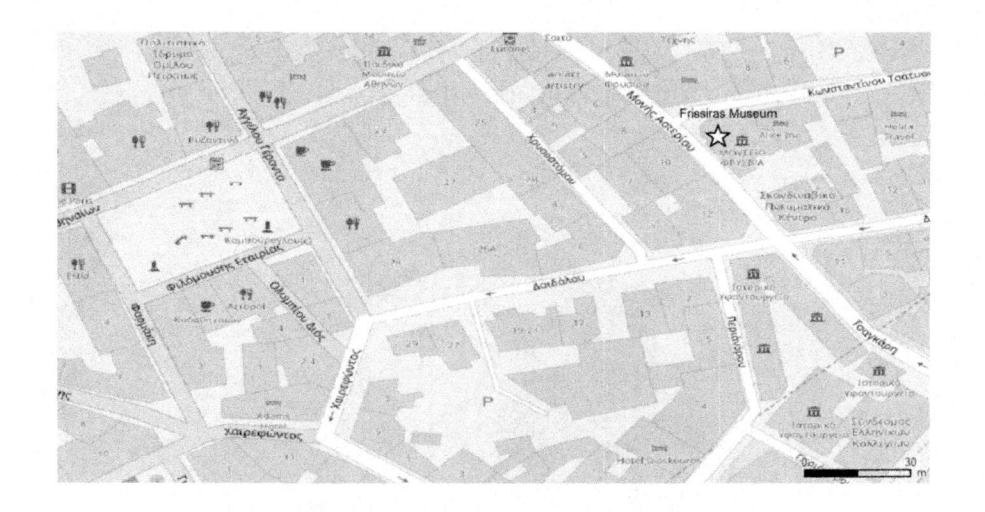

4. Monument of Lysicrates. The miniature library

The monument of Lysicrates today. Lysikratous Square, Plaka, Athens

In Lysikratous square, very close to Frissiras Museum, you will see the monument of Lysicrates. In case you wonder why it figures on our list, since it's an ancient monument and well known by guidebooks, there are two reasons for its presence here: first, its connection with the previous sight, which demonstrates how ancient monuments were used as models for modern buildings, without having any relation with them. And then, its history after ancient times.

In 335-334 BC, Lysicrates, sponsor (choregos in Greek) of a play at the theatrical contest of the Great Dionysia (in honour of Dionysus), built the monument to celebrate his victory. This is why it is called a choragic monument. On it, a bronze tripod was placed. The same was done with all choragic monuments that were starting from the Theatre of Dionysus and were arrayed on the same street. This is why the street's name was Tripods Street, the same as today (Tripodon). For obvious reasons, the monument depicted a mythological scene with Dionysus. Tyrrhenian pirates have captured him, not knowing who he is. He punishes them by turning them into dolphins.

The monument became known as the lantern of Diogenes, perhaps because of its shape. It was said that the philosopher Diogenes went about with a lantern, searching to find a (real) man. Of course, he had nothing to do with the monument.

But what is very peculiar about this monument is its more recent history. In 1669, French Capuchin monks came to Athens (it's not them who invented the cappuccino coffee. The coffee got its name from their characteristic brown cap). The Capuchins founded a monastery there and turned the monument into a library. This is why it survived, unlike all its neighbouring choragic monuments. The building was extensively reproduced in the 18th century and became known worldwide. Even 'improved' versions of it appeared in many places, even in the United States or Australia.

The Capuchins made the first topographic plan of Athens, in 1670. In 1818, the monk Francis planted in the gardens of the monastery the first tomato plants in Greece. The monastery burned down during the Revolution and the monument remained in ruins for many years, until it was restored in 1876-1887.

The monument of Lysicrates in the court of the monastery of the Capuchins, 1762, James Stuart and Nicholas Revett. The monks hosted Lord Byron (public domain work, {{PD-1923}})

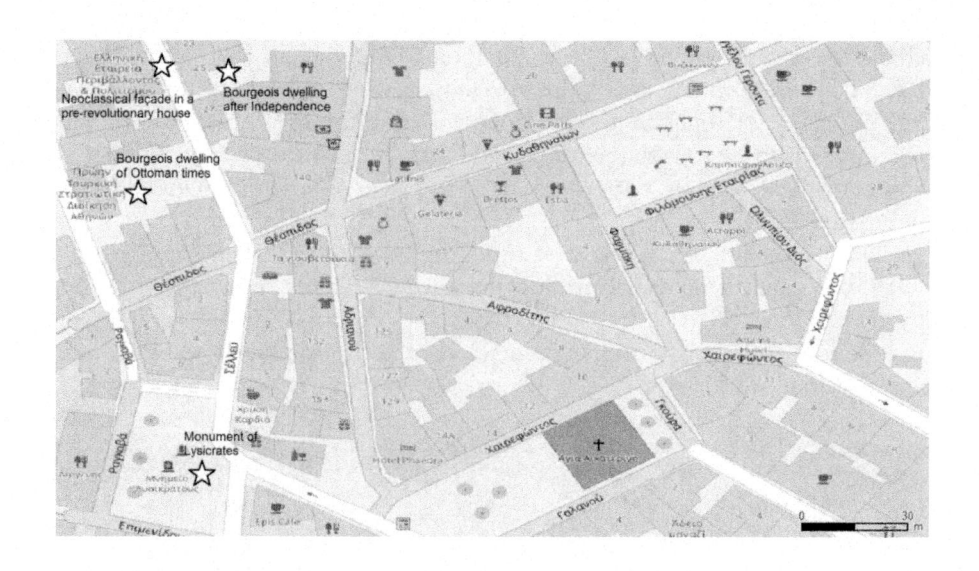

5. A bourgeois dwelling of Ottoman times
The survival of ancient houses

A traditional house of the 18th century

From Lysikratous Square, we will take Tripodon Street. Immediately afterwards, we will see on the left a typical house of the 18th century. This is a characteristic house of the centuries that preceded Independence, before the advent of classicism. You should imagine Athens and all the other towns of Greece having houses like this.

Here you see the backyard, with the hayat (loggia). The hayat served as a corridor and balcony. As a corridor, it allowed communication between rooms. As a balcony, it allowed one to benefit from the sun during the winter months, under the protection of a roof. In fact, this type of house dates from ancient times, since it was perfectly adapted to the Mediterranean climate, which permitted to spend a lot of time outdoors. The only main difference is in the glass panes, but these were added after Independence when it became possible to produce them in Greece. Thus, the corridor became even more useful, since it could be used in the sunny but cold days of winter as a sitting-room.

In the next picture, you see a house from Makrinitsa, on Mount Pelion.

This is the typical upper-class house of Northern Greece and depicts the difference from the South. The northern parts of Greece were wealthier in Byzantine and Ottoman times, so houses were made of more solid materials and could have a more imposing aspect. Moreover, the climate in the North was much less lenient, which led to a more 'introverted' architecture.

A house in Makrinitsa, Mount Pelion. A typical example of housing in Northern Greece, much wealthier than the South, but also with a less Mediterranean climate

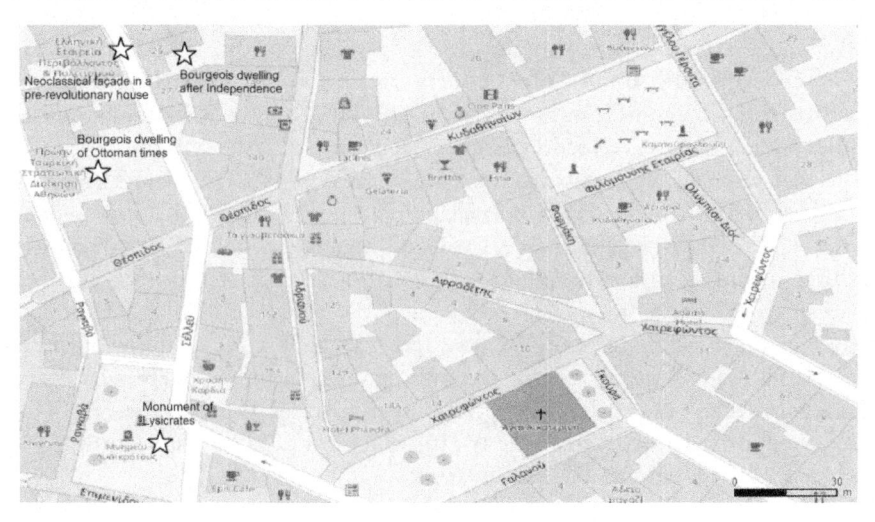

6. A bourgeois dwelling after Independence
Neoclassical in the front, traditional in the back

A neoclassical facade in a traditional house

Almost opposite the previous house, always in Tripodon Street, we will see a strange sight, which, however, is not rare at all. This house was built after the Revolution and is a typical transitional sample: from the architecture of the Ottoman times to the architecture of Independence. The facade, seen from the street, is the official part of the house. This is neoclassical because classicism symbolized two things: Europeanization and connection to the ancient past. Exactly what liberated Greece desired. The rest of the house, however, is traditional. It has an inner courtyard and a hayat (loggia). This architecture was adapted to the Greek climate and served the daily needs better.

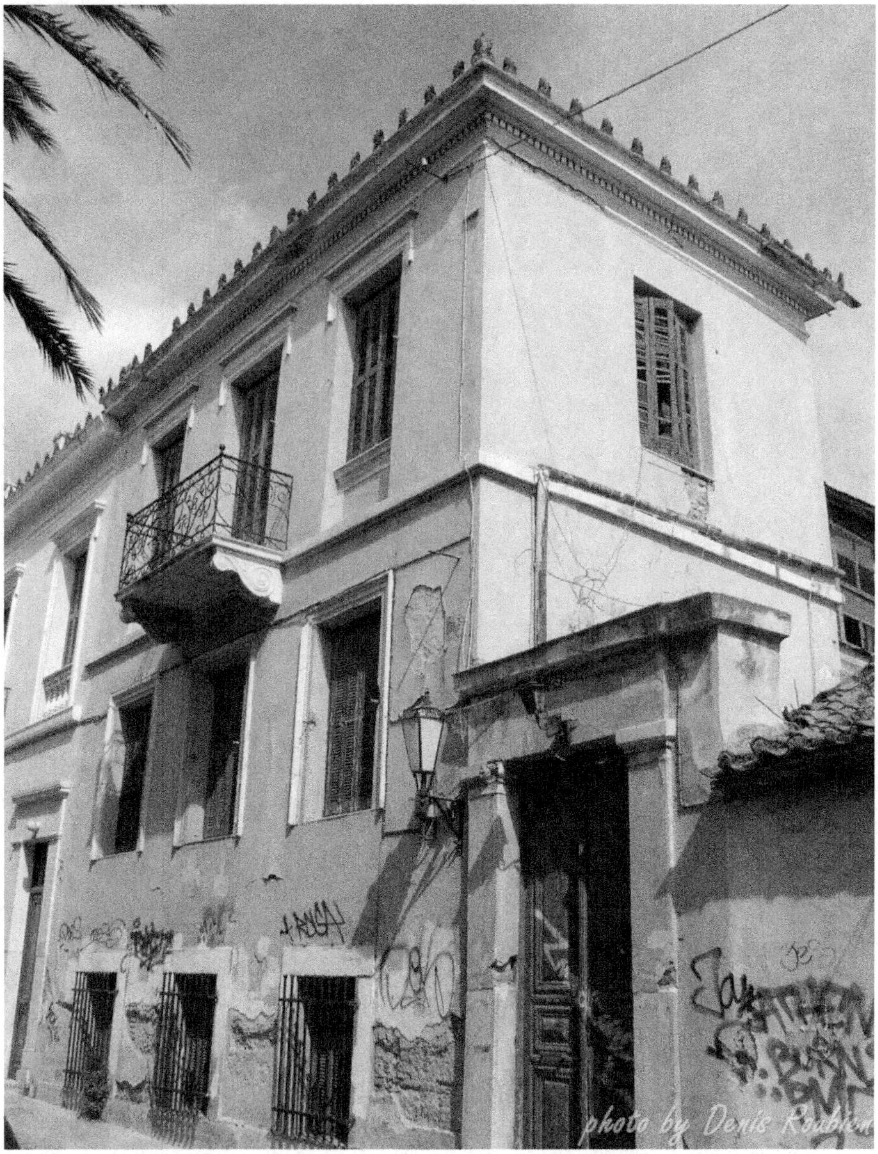
photo by Denis Roubien

7. A neoclassical façade in a pre-revolutionary house

Just farther up Tripodon Street, almost opposite the previous house, you will see another one. The neoclassical facade hides a bourgeois pre-revolutionary house. It's similar to the previous one, except that here they added the 'modern' neoclassical facade to an older building of Ottoman times. For the same reasons: Europeanization and connection to the ancient past.

You may observe that this facade is much simpler than the Frissiras Museum. That's because neoclassical houses of the first decades after Independence were simpler for two reasons: one was that time's more moderated views on the use of ancient motives in modern buildings. The other was just that technology was very rudimentary in the newborn State and it was not possible to make the rich decoration of later decades. This is why in Athens you will see neoclassical buildings of all types: from so simple ones that they can barely be called neoclassical, up to excessively decorated ones.

This house is of particular interest, because, in the basement, you can see ancient walls and other findings, testifying once more of this city's complex and multi-layered character. It's possible to descend to the basement since today the house is the seat of the 'Hellenic Society for the Protection of Environment and the Cultural Heritage'.

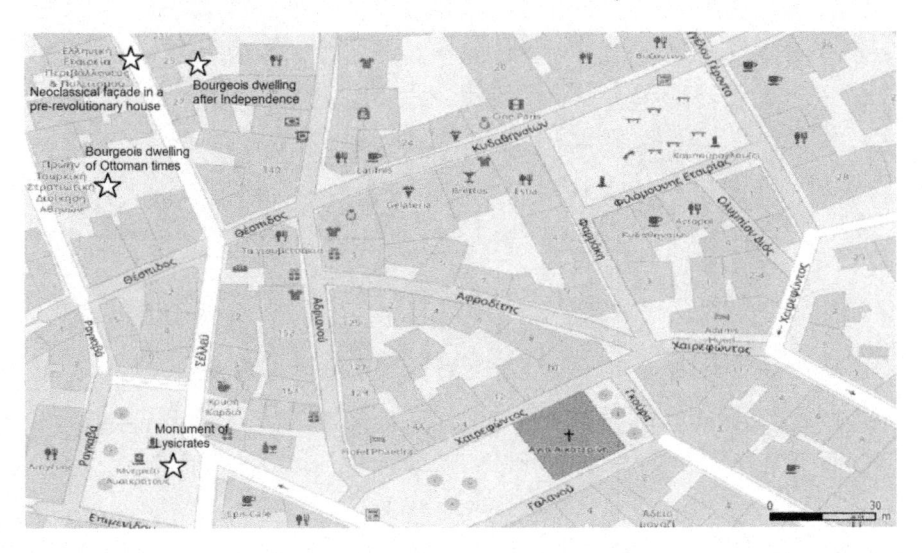

The neoclassical facade hides well a pre-revolutionary house. A typical example of the simple classicism of the first decades

8. Saint Nicholas Ragava
How to distinguish a Byzantine church

A little bit farther up Tripodon Street, we stumble upon the church of Saint Nicholas Ragava. Its name, like in the case of most Byzantine and post-Byzantine churches of Athens, indicates the name of the family that undertook its construction.

Old churches of Athens are either Byzantine (before 1204, when Athens fell to the crusaders of the 4rth crusade), or post-Byzantine, namely, from the times of foreign domination, either Western European or Ottoman (from 1456 to Independence). It's fairly easy to distinguish them. Byzantine churches were built as representatives of the official religion. Therefore, although small (as Athens was a small town), they have an elegant and elaborated external decoration. They also have a dome, a very important feature for the Orthodox religious architecture, as it symbolizes heaven.

From the time of Western domination, there are no churches and practically no monuments, a fact that depicts the very low state of Athens at that time. The churches of Ottoman times differ from the Byzantine ones and are easy to distinguish. Since now they represent the religion not of the rulers but of the conquered population, they are of poorer construction quality and don't have a dome. The latter was prohibited, as it added height to the building, which was not accepted, since the mosques, representing the rulers' religion, had to stand out clearly. We will see a sample of this architecture later.

The interesting thing here is that, next to the 11th-century main Byzantine body of very decorative exterior elements, we see a facade that has nothing to do with it. This is —or was- the case of many churches in Athens, who, after Independence, underwent extensive works of enlargement, in order to include the increased number of parishioners, due to the new capital's continuous increase of population. Since the dominating style was classicism, the additions were made in that style, regardless of the lack of homogeneity that this entailed.

In many cases, the additions were removed in the 20th century, when Byzantine architecture gained the acknowledgement it deserved. But not in all cases, either because it was impossible to restore the initial form, or because the needs were too acute to diminish the church's size.

Saint Nicholas Ragava. The very decorated exterior is very typical of Athenian Byzantine churches

In this particular church, you will see something unusual, if you walk in. Immediately after the entrance, there is a bell hanging in the interior. It's kept there because of its historical value. During the Ottoman domination, churches were not allowed to have bells. The only exception was Saint Nicholas. It was, therefore, its bell that announced the liberation of Athens in 1833, when the Turkish guard delivered the city to the representatives of the newly elected King Otto.

Saint Nicholas Ragava. Here it's obvious that the facade is a subsequent neoclassical addition

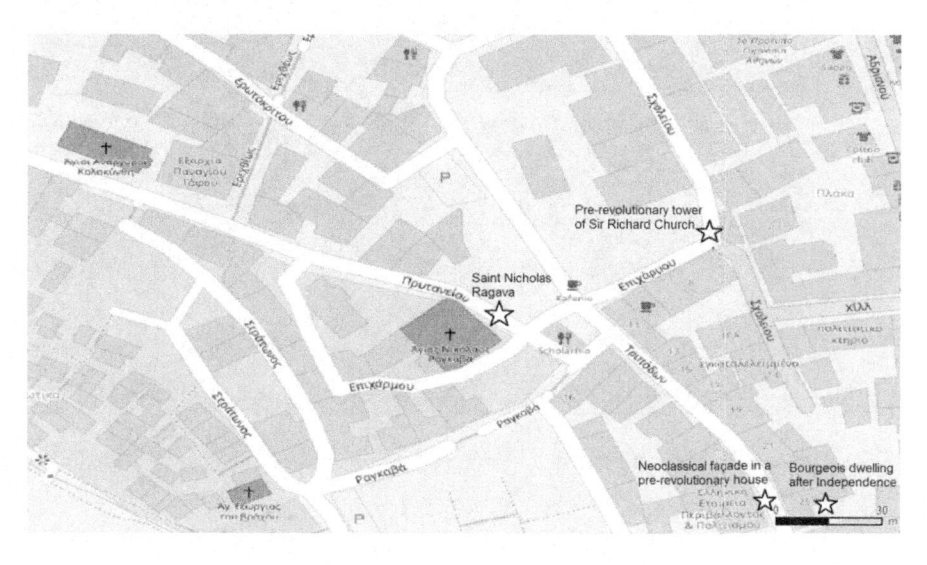

Saint Nicholas Ragava. All the front part (including the bell tower) was added after Independence

9. The last pre-revolutionary tower in Athens

The house of Sir Richard Church, the only remaining sample of pre-revolutionary tower-houses

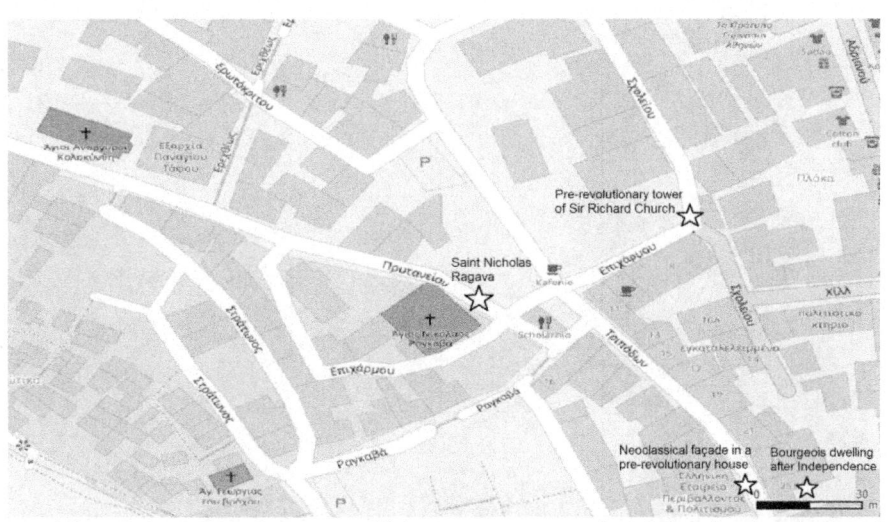

After Saint Nicholas, you will have to turn to the right. At the angle of

Epicharmou and Scholeiou Streets, you will see an unusual building. It was the residence of the British General Sir Richard Church, who was commander of the Greek forces in the Greek Revolution. It was the property of the English historian George Finlay, who lived nearby. It is the only tower-house of Ottoman times surviving in Athens. According to the sources, there were many such buildings in Ottoman Athens. Their appearance testifies to the need for protection against invasions.

10. The last mansion of pre-revolutionary Athens

Benizelos mansion, the oldest house in Athens

A little farther to the right, after the house of General Church, you will see Benizelos mansion. The entrance is from Adrianou Street. Here we see the rear part, which is more interesting since the facade is hidden behind a very tall wall. It dates from the 16th and the 17th centuries and is the only subsisting mansion of Ottoman Athens. It's also the oldest house in the Greek capital. The time of its construction makes it one of the very few links between Byzantine and post-Byzantine secular architecture since very few houses dating earlier than the 18th century remain in the whole country.

But research has shown that this building type is much older and you must imagine Greek cities, at least since the last centuries of Byzantium, having a lot of such houses. This type reflects the change of circumstances, when the precarious state of the Byzantine Empire and the oppression during Ottoman domination gave the houses, at least those of the upper class, who had something to protect, a fortified character. The sahnisi (enclosed balcony) increased space and created a bright living room (oda).

Benizelos mansion. The sahnisi (enclosed balcony) increased space and created a bright living room (oda)

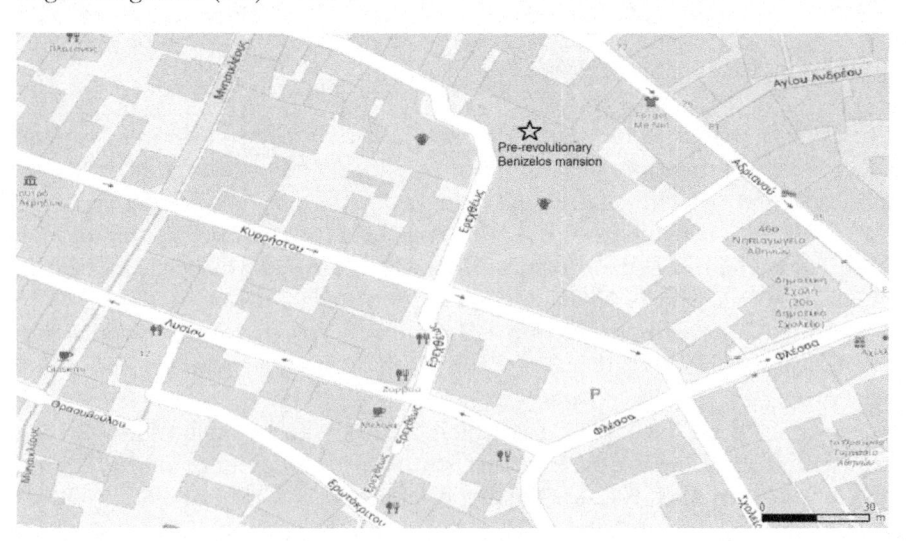

11. Gorgoepikoos (small cathedral)
A link between ancient times and the Middle Ages

After the Benizelos mansion, if you go farther to the right, you will find yourself in Mitropoleos Square (Cathedral Square). There, just next to the cathedral, a building of the 19th century with no special merits, you will see one of the many Byzantine churches of Athens. Only this one is different from the others. Because it is entirely built of remains of ancient buildings.

It's easy to distinguish the medieval buildings made of ancient materials. Whenever you see huge stones among much smaller ones, the huge ones are ancient and come from that very spot. In the Middle Ages, when the Roman routes disappeared, for lack of maintenance, stones could only be transferred on mules, so they had to be small. To limit the trouble, whenever it was possible, they used the remains of ancient buildings, which were extremely abundant.

Gorgoepikoos. Perhaps the most elegant old church of Athens

Gorgoepikoos. A church made entirely of ancient materials

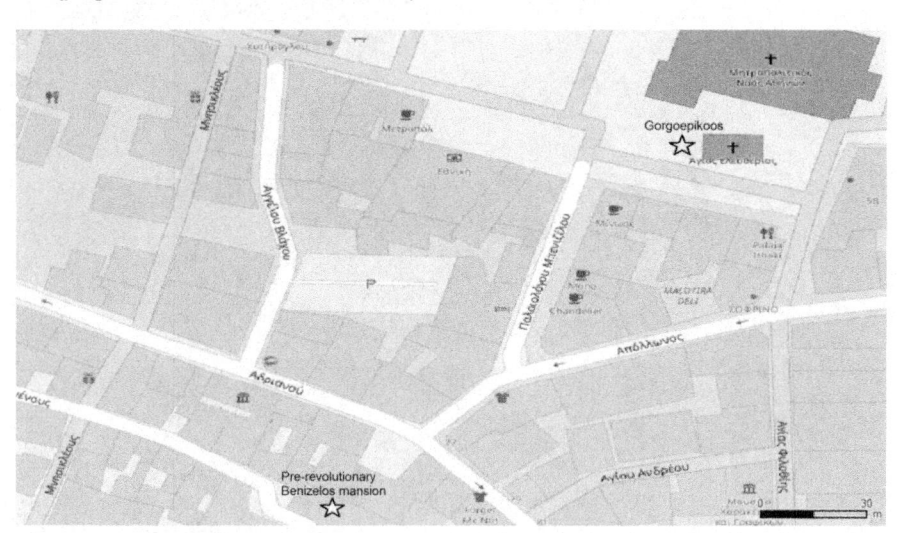

12. Saints Anarghyri. Religious architecture after Byzantium

If you go back towards Saint Nicholas Ragava and a little farther beyond its facade, on Erechtheos Street, you will see the church of Saints Anarghyri Kolokynthi. Built around 1600 and belonging to a priest named Kolokynthis, it's a typical example of religious architecture in Athens under the Ottomans: low and without a dome, since, as we said, these two features were compulsory to make churches lower than mosques. Like most other Athenian churches, it underwent neoclassical interventions of 'modernization', which include the bell tower. The church is a dependency of the Holy Sepulchre of Jerusalem (Orthodox Patriarchate of Jerusalem).

Saints Anarghyri Kolokynthi. A typical example of a church of Ottoman times, low, without a dome, and of poor materials, reflecting the change of circumstances for the Christians

13. The house of the creator of modern Athens

Museum of the Athens University. Neoclassical details on a traditional layout

A little farther up and to the left, in Tholou Street, you will see the Museum of the Athens University. It was originally the house of Stamatios Kleanthes, the architect who prepared the first plan of Athens. It was the plan we saw at the beginning of our tour, the one with the three grids surrounding a triangle linked to the old city.

This was a house of Ottoman times and Kleanthes gave it a neoclassical character. Later, it housed the High School and then the University, before the grandiose neoclassical building of Panepistimiou Street was constructed.

Museum of the Athens University. The back courtyard

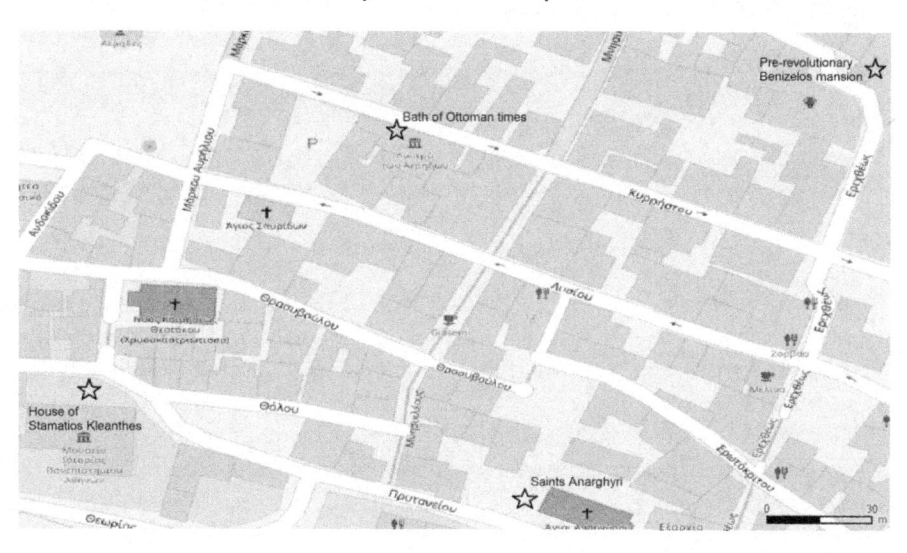

14. The last bath of Ottoman times in Athens

Below Tholou Street and parallel to it is Kyrristou Street. There you will find the only subsisting bath of Ottoman Athens. Now it's a museum worth seeing.

Ottoman bath. The rear part with the glass skylights

Don't be fooled by the neoclassical facade. Like in so many other buildings (as we saw), it was added after Independence. On the back, you can see the glass skylights of the roof, revealing that this building is not quite what it seems.

The baths were an important place of social interaction, especially for the women of Ottoman times, who didn't have other occasions to leave their houses. Thus, the visit to the hammam was a ritual. The 'loutrikia' or 'loutrika', the total of the items used by the bride in the bath, are often mentioned in the premarital donations of the groom to the bride. Two Britons, Lady Cravin and Lady Elgin write impressed by the voluptuous Greek and Turkish women with obese bodies who were eating kataifs, drinking soft drinks, singing and dancing, playing the tambourine, the guitar, and the oud. In the event of a fight, clogs and cups belonging to the 'loutrikia' were hurled at the opponents.

Ottoman bath. The facade

15. The Roman Forum

Kyrristou Street took its name from the nearby Kyrristos Clock, best known as the Tower of the Winds. The Horologion of Kyrristos, just out of the Roman Forum, was built by astronomer Andronikos in the 1st century BC. The winds are sculpted on the sides. Outside there were sundials, while in the interior there was a hydraulic clock. The hydraulic clock worked as follows: there were two tanks on two levels. The water from the source of Klepsydra on the Acropolis reached the top tank and from there to the bottom one where there was a float connected with a bronze chain. As it was going up with the water level, it was moving the chain, which was rotating the clock mechanism in the centre of the tower. Every 24 hours they were tuning the clock by emptying the small tank.

The Tower of the Winds was transformed in the early Christian era into a church or baptistery of a neighbouring church. In the 15th century, Ciriaco d'Ancona mentions it as the temple of Aeolus, while an anonymous traveller mentions it as a church. In the 18th century, it was used as a tekke, namely, a gathering place, of dervishes. The dervishes are Muslim ascetics, engaging in ritualistic mystical dances, where they can rotate unceasingly for a long time. The dervishes used the monument until 1828 and prevented Lord Elgin from taking it along with the sculptures of the Acropolis, as he intended, as they considered it sacred.

The Roman Forum, dating from the Augustus era, was for centuries the city's commercial centre, as the Wheat Market, the heart of Ottoman Athens, was also here. You will see a U-shaped colonnade, with an entrance (the Gate of Athena Archegetis). Across it, there are little neoclassical houses, typical of Plaka. But what needs an explanation is the one thing it's impossible to guess.

The apparently U-shaped building was a closed rectangle, with an internal court and a colonnade running along its four interior sides. By a strange fate, the southern part was preserved, while the northern part disappeared completely. In its place houses were built, replaced many times since. Those we see today date from the 19th century.

What happened makes the comprehension of modern Athens more difficult than you might think. Because something similar happened also to the building which stood just next and parallel to the Roman Forum: the Library of Hadrian, which was a rectangle similar to the Forum, although much more luxurious. It also had an internal court with a colonnade running along its sides. In fact, it was built by Emperor Hadrian as a counterpart to the older building.

Which is exactly what you can't see today. Because the Library of Hadrian lost its southern part, exactly the one close to the Roman Forum.

Here also houses took the place of the once grandiose monument. The houses you see behind the ones opposite the colonnade of the Forum. Therefore, today, instead of having two rectangles parallel to one another and of similar dimensions, we have two U-shaped buildings facing the cluster of houses separating them. You will understand this better when you move to the Library of Hadrian. But before doing so, there are two neglected sights worth taking a look at.

The Roman Forum. In the front the remaining colonnade and in the background, from left to right, the houses separating the ruins of the Forum from those of the Library of Hadrian, the Ottoman Fethiye Mosque, and the Roman Tower of the Winds

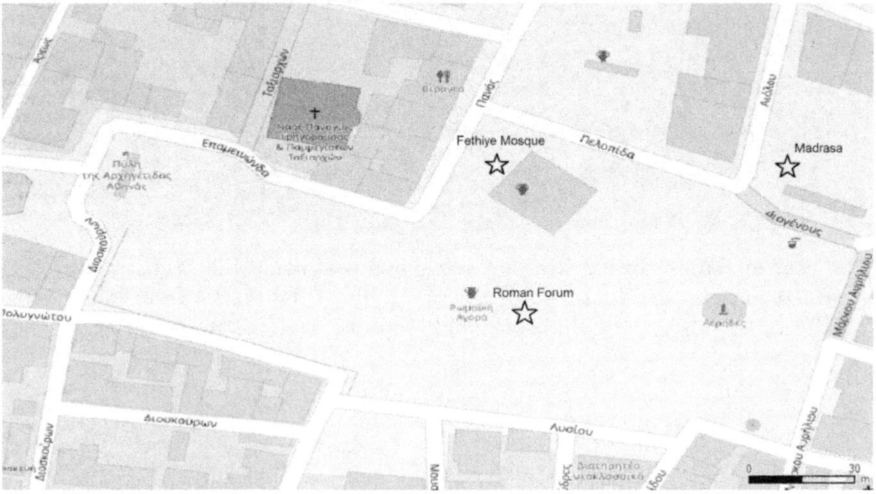
Fethiye Mosque
Madrasa
Roman Forum
Επαμεινώνδα
Πελοπίδα
Διογένους
Διοσκούρων
Λυσίου
Πανός
Αιόλου
Ταξιαρχών
Πολυγνώτου
0
30

16. The Madrasa

The entrance of the Madrasa, the only remaining part of this Muslim religious school

The first one is the Madrasa, or rather what remains of it. It was a Muslim religious school under the Ottomans. After Independence, it was turned into a jail, which accelerated its decay. Thus, it was demolished at the beginning of the 20th century. What remains is just the entrance, but it is worth a look since it has original decorative motives, making it a very different sight from the others.

The Madrasa can be seen in the background

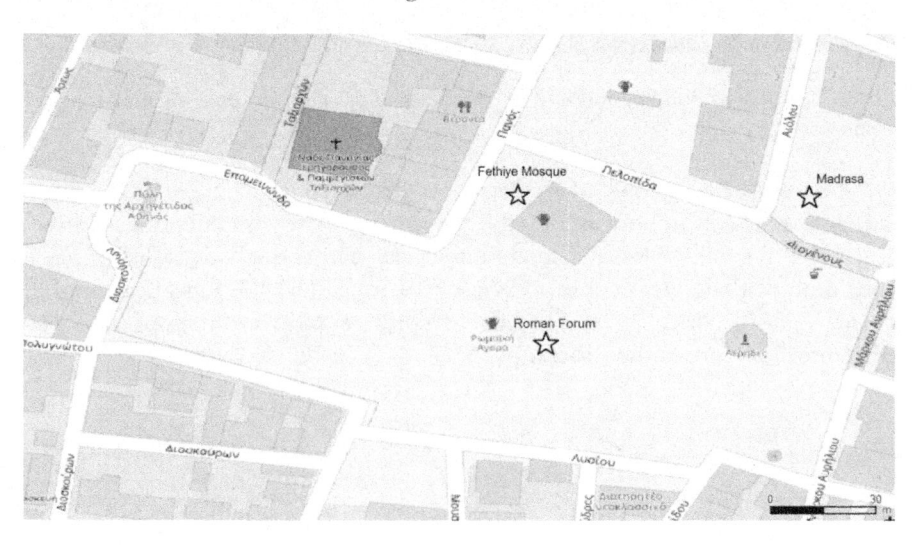

17. The Fethiye Mosque

The Fethiye Mosque, built on the ruins of a Byzantine basilica

Just close to the Madrasa and in the archaeological site of the Roman Forum is the Fethiye Mosque (Mosque of the Conqueror). Its name is due to a tradition according to which it was built by the Ottoman Sultan Mehmed the Conqueror, the same who conquered Constantinople, when he conquered Athens, in 1456. However, recent research has revealed that it dates from the 17th century. In any case, it is interesting as a vestige of an obscure past, even more so because it was built on the remains of a Byzantine basilica, which can be seen around the building.

photo by Denis Roubien

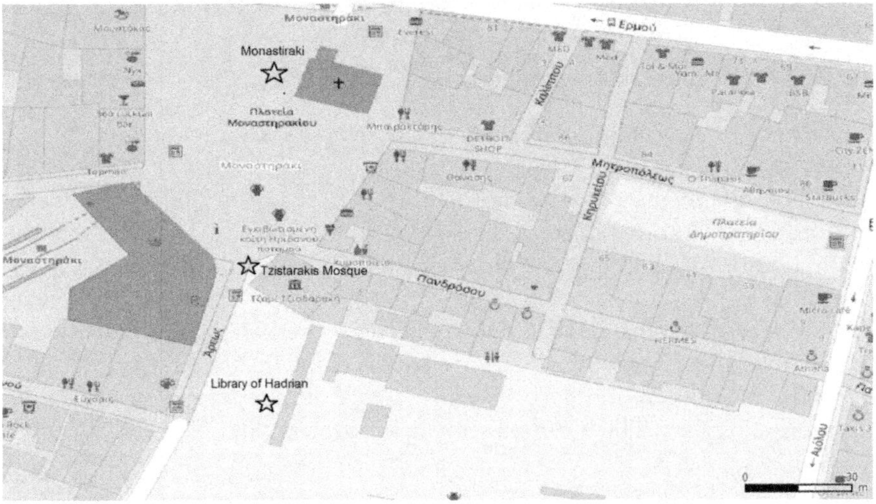
Monastiraki
Tzistarakis Mosque
Library of Hadrian
Ερμού
Μητροπόλεως
Πανδρόσου
Αιόλου
0
30
m

18. The library of Hadrian and the church on the stairs

The Library of Hadrian. On the wall just on the left of the entrance, a mural painting remains from the Byzantine church of Saint Asomatos on the Stairs. In the background, the Tzistarakis Mosque

After that, you can move to the Library of Hadrian and see for yourself the relation it had with the Roman Forum. Hadrian's Library, built in 132 AD, was one of the Roman Emperor's gifts to the city he loved, as a great admirer of Greek civilization. The building followed the typical layout of a Roman forum, having only one entrance with a propylon of the Corinthian order, a high surrounding wall with protruding niches at its long sides, an inner courtyard surrounded by columns, and a decorative oblong pool in the middle. The library was on the eastern side. Adjoining halls were used as reading rooms, and the corners served as lecture halls. The library was seriously damaged during the raid of the Heruli of 267 and repaired by the prefect Herculius in AD 407–412. In the 5th century, the quatrefoil building of an Early Christian church was constructed in the centre of the peristyle court. After its destruction, a three-aisled basilica was erected on its ruins in the 7th century, which was in turn superseded by the single-aisled church of Megali Panaghia, in the 11th century. In Ottoman times, the Voivodalik, the voivode's dwelling, was built on its ruins. Under King Otto, this became a barracks and then was demolished to make the library appear.

In the 12th century, Saint Asomatos (Archangel Michael) a very little church, was built against the library's facade, on the left of the entrance. As it was built on the library's steps, it was known as 'Aghios Asomatos sta skalia' (Saint Asomatos on the stairs). It was a very good example of the utilitarian way ancient monuments were seen in the Middle Ages. The ruined library's standing wall was just a good background for the church to be built, saving materials, money, and time since only three walls had to be built. In the 19th century, when ancient monuments were seen as absolutely superior to subsequent ones, the church was demolished. But the mural painting of the back can still be seen on the library's wall, as a fascinating example of this town's multi-layered history.

Four layers of history. From the foreground to the background: the Library of Hadrian, the Tzistarakis Mosque, and the Byzantine church of the Dormition of the Virgin (Pantanassa), with its neoclassical bell tower

19. The Tzistarakis Mosque

Tzistarakis Mosque

Just next to the Library of Hadrian, on Monastiraki Square, is the Tzistarakis Mosque, now the Ceramics Museum. It was named after the 18th-century governor of Athens who built it. It's interesting to note the difference of this building of elegant details from the rough 17th-century Fethiye Mosque. Now the Ottoman Empire is influenced by Western classicism and the building's decorative elements clearly reflect this evolution.

It is said that Tzistarakis melted in a furnace a column of the temple of Olympian Zeus to make good quality lime for his mosque. This caused the wrath of the Athenians, who believed that demons were hiding under the ancient monuments. There followed a fatal epidemic and the Athenians thought it was caused by the demons hidden under the column and released by its destruction. This exhausted their patience, as they suffered much from Tzistarakis. So they denounced his arbitrariness to the sultan and Tzistarakis was deposed. This reinforced the faith in the misfortune brought about by the destruction of the monuments.

The images around the Tzistarakis Mosque demonstrate the survival of the oriental bazaar which was exactly here, a continuation of the ancient market represented by the Roman Forum and the Ancient Agora, situated just next to it. In fact, that has always been the commercial (and not only) heart of Athens.

The new plan of Athens took into account this reality since Monastiraki square is the intersection point of the base and the bisector of the triangle that forms the new city's spine (see the plan at the beginning).

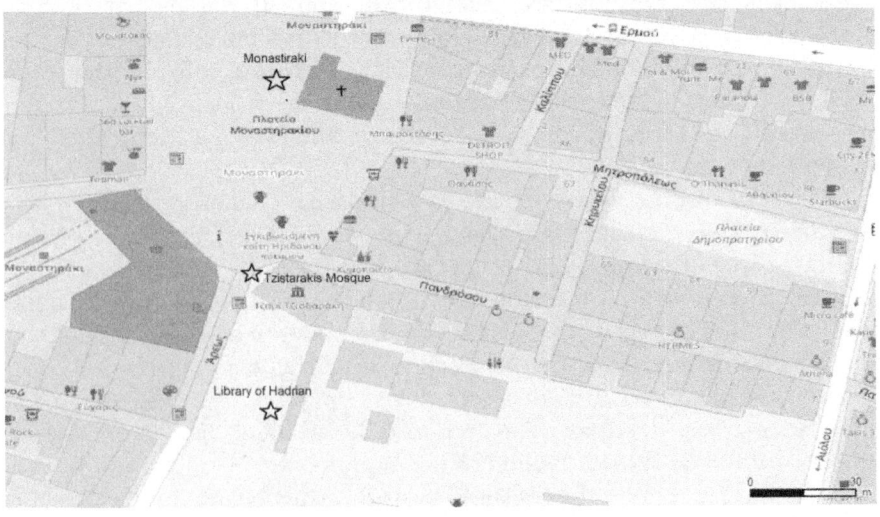

20. Monastiraki. The great monastery that became small

And if you wonder about this square's name, which means 'little monastery', the answer lies opposite the mosque. The 10th-century church of the Dormition of the Virgin (Pantanassa), was part of a monastery known as Mega Monastiri (Great Monastery). When a fire destroyed the whole complex, sparing only the church, the name changed to Monastiraki (Little Monastery).

Apart from that, the church is interesting as a very good example of this city's multiple layers. The level of the church, much lower than that of the square, testifies of the continuous disasters that always left ruins, on which the town was rebuilt again and again. Thus, the level of each monument reveals its age.

To corroborate that, you just have to look through the glass covers of the square downwards. Then you will see the river Eridanus, which runs under the square and was transformed into a gutter by the Romans. If you descend into the Metro Station Monastiraki just underneath, you will be able to see its interesting network.

Monastiraki. A 10th-century church with a neoclassical bell tower

21. Saint Eleousa: From a church to a courthouse

Library of the Archdiocese of Athens. Who could imagine it hides a church on the inside?

If you go beyond Monastiraki Square, across Hermes Street (Ermou), the triangle's base, and a bit to the left, from Athena Street (Athinas), the triangle's bisector, you will find yourself in Aghias Eleousis Street, in the district of Psyrri. There you will see the Library of the Archdiocese of Athens. Previously, it was the Assizes, a work of Christian Hansen, a 19th-century Danish architect, who also designed the Athens University.

What is particularly interesting and original with this building, justifying its inclusion in this list, it's that it resulted from the conversion of the post-Byzantine church of Saint Eleousa (Virgin Mary of the Mercy), dating perhaps from the 17th century. Its sanctuary still exists in the building's rear part and you can see it if you enter it.

Another very particular feature is that the doorway of the entrance copies the doorway of the north porch of the Erechtheion. Since this building dates from 1835, just after Athens became the capital of Greece, it's the very first attempt to copy the ancient monuments in modern buildings. This gives it a special historical value.

Next to Saint Eleousa, at 14, Aghias Theklas Street was the house of Teresa Makri. Teresa or Theresia Makri was an Athenian beauty, the eldest of the three daughters of Prokopios Makris, consul of Great Britain. She was born in 1797 and baptized in Saint Eleousa, her family's parish church. At her home, Teresa, only thirteen years old, met Lord Byron in 1810. Her widowed mother made a living renting rooms to travellers. The three-month stay of Byron was accompanied by a romance. The poet fell madly in love with Teresa, who became his muse. For her, he wrote the poem 'The Maid of Athens'.

In 1829, Teresa married the English officer James Black, with whom she had four children. Teresa was of astounding beauty, highly educated. She spoke foreign languages and published with her sister a dictionary in Corfu, where her family had found refuge during the Revolution. At the end of her life she had difficult days. In 1872, French composer Charles Gounod composed a work titled 'Maid of Athens', sending all the proceeds from the concert to Teresa to help her. Teresa died in Athens in 1875. The Benaki Museum holds her red fez with the golden tassel next to a desk of Byron's.

Library of the Archdiocese of Athens. The doorway of the entrance copies the Erechtheion

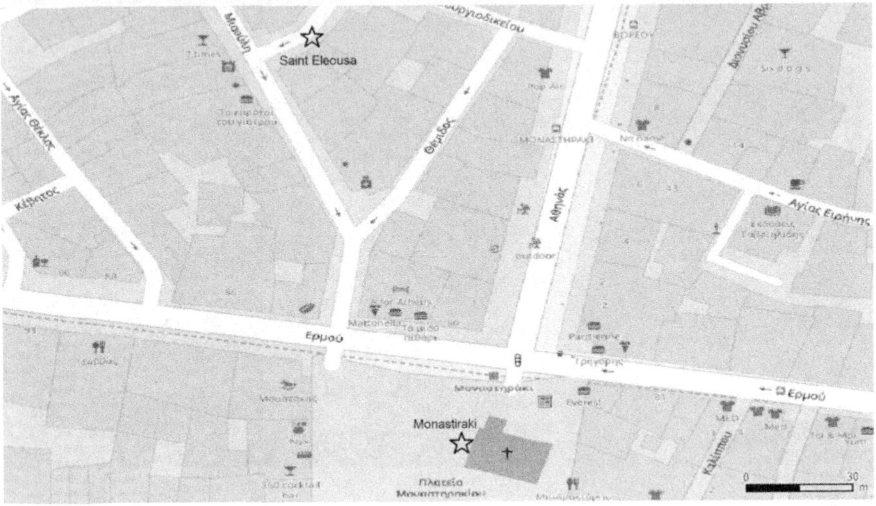
Saint Eleousa
Monastiraki
Ερμού
Αθηνάς
Θεμιδος
Κέβητος
Μιαούλη
Πλατεία Μοναστηρακίου

22. Academy of Athens. The exception on the list

The central part of the Academy of Athens copies the northern porch of the Erechtheion, marking the summit of neoclassical architecture in Greece

You will undoubtedly remark that this sight is very different from the previous ones. In fact, it's the most grandiose neoclassical edifice of Athens. But it's precisely this that will show you the great change that the Greek capital underwent in the 50 years that separate this building from the previous one. The former is characteristic of a poor country struggling to become a member of the European family and re-connect with its ancient roots. Thus, they only could copy a part of the Erechtheion's entrance. The latter is proud proof of the great progress made with a lot of effort. Therefore, here the whole Erechtheion was copied, with its elaborate and luxurious marble construction and its sumptuous and resplendent décor. There could not be a better example of the country's and the city's evolution in half a century.

Next to the Academy, along an axis forming the boundaries between the old and obsolete town (in the eyes of that time) and the new modern European capital, you will see many other majestic neoclassical edifices. And here begins our second itinerary…

23. The modern city of Athens
The 'Monumental Axis'
and its relationship with the antiquities

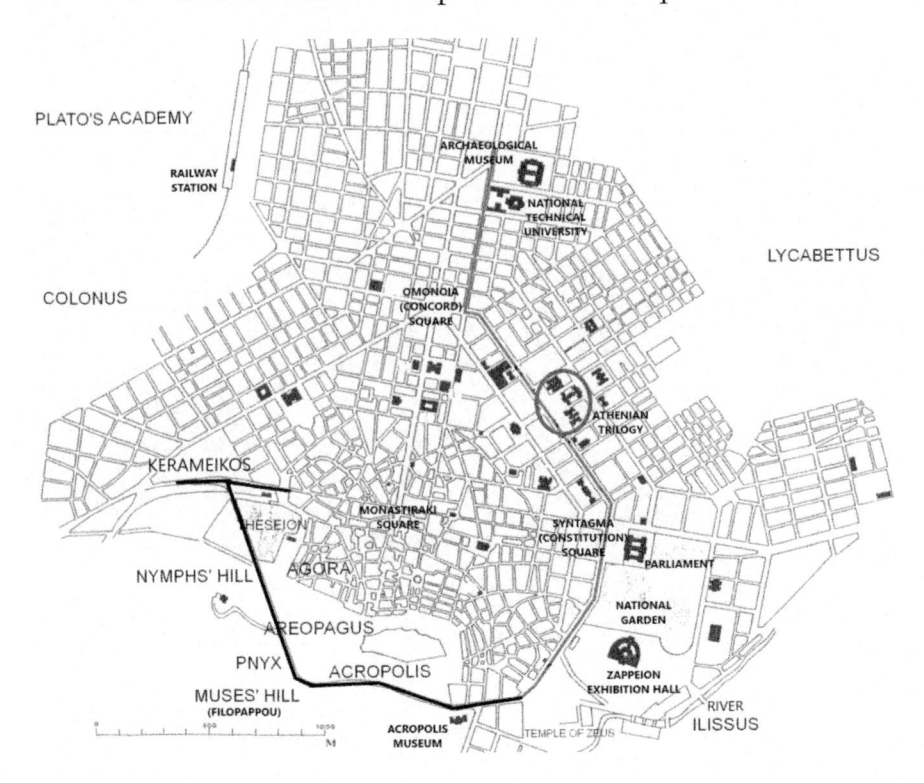

Athens in the 19th century (drawn by the author). The 'Monumental Axis', indicated by the grey line on the right part of the plan, is the proposed itinerary in case you want to discover the main monuments of neoclassical Athens, the modern city created from 1833 onwards as the capital of the newly founded Greek State. The black line on the lower and left part of the plan indicates the 'Great Promenade', the pedestrian zone created in 2001-2004 to unite the archaeological sites of Athens. All these sites are indicated in regular letters. Sites and buildings of modern Athens are indicated in bold letters

This chapter proposes an itinerary starting at approximately the same point as the previous one and more precisely at the junction of the avenues Amalias and Dionysiou Areopagitou (where the grey line meets the black line on the plan). This time, we will discover the neoclassical city created from 1833 onwards as an extension of the old town we discovered previously. This modern city would be the capital of the new Greek State, founded in 1830. The main monuments I suggest you see in order to have a complete idea are the following: the Zappeion Exhibition Hall, close to Amalias Avenue, the Parliament, in Syntagma Square, at the junction between Amalias Avenue and Panepistimiou Street, the Athenian Trilogy in Panepistimiou Street (Academy of Athens, University of Athens, National Library), and the two buildings in Patision Street, namely, the National Technical University (Polytechnic) and the National Archaeological Museum. These three avenues, Amalias, Panepistimiou, and Patision, form what is sometimes referred to as the 'Monumental Axis' of Athens. At the end of this itinerary, you can visit the National Archaeological Museum, which houses the greatest collection of ancient Greek art in the world.

And now, let's see how this 'Monumental Axis' was created and what is unique in its creation... The monumental neoclassical buildings of Athens, although representing infinitesimal volumes in today's enormous metropolis, contrary to their complete domination in the time of their construction, have not lost their symbolical power as major elements of the Greek capital's urban landscape. However, while the initial plans predicted a very balanced distribution of the capital's monumental buildings within the urban fabric, according to all rational principles of their time, today's situation shows a very clear displacement of those buildings along the aforementioned axis. This includes most of the monumental buildings of the Greek capital: in Patision Street, the Archaeological Museum and the Polytechnic; in Panepistimiou Street (now officially Eleftheriou Venizelou), the Council of State (former Arsakeion School for Girls), the National Library, the University, the Academy of Athens, the Catholic Cathedral, the Numismatic Museum (former mansion of the famous archaeologist Heinrich Schliemann and most luxurious private building of 19th-century Athens), the Bank of Greece; in Amalias Avenue, the Parliament (former Royal Palace) with the National Garden, and the Zappeion Exhibition Hall.

That change from a triangular layout to a linear one is the result of a process reflecting the essence of modern Athens' creation, after Independence: an effort to satisfy the two main aims set in the process of creating the new Greek State: its reconnection with the ancient past and its entry in the family of the civilized nations of Western Europe. Namely, replacing the provincial Ottoman town with a modern European capital, but at the same time taking advantage of the presence of its ancient monuments of international fame and creating a city unique in the world.

The Zappeion Exhibition Hall (1873-1888), by Theophil Hansen. Below, the peristyle of the internal courtyard

The Royal Palace of Athens (1836-1842), by Friedrich von Gärtner, in Syntagma (Constitution) Square, in a 19th-century engraving. Now it houses the Parliament

The Academy of Athens (1859-1885), by Theophil Hansen, part of the 'Athenian Trilogy'. The supreme cultural institution of Greece

Above, the old building of the University of Athens (1839-1864), by Christian Hansen, now housing only the rectorate. The oldest building of the 'Athenian Trilogy'. Below, the old building of the National Library (1885-1902), by Theophil Hansen, also part of the 'Athenian Trilogy'. Now the National Library is housed in the complex of the Stavros Niarchos Foundation, one of the most important cultural institutions in modern Greece, which I recommend you visit

The National Technical University of Athens, or Polytechnic (1862-1876), one of the most important institutions of Higher Education in Greece, was founded in 1837

The National Archaeological Museum of Athens (1866-1889). It houses the greatest collection of ancient Greek art in the world

According to that concept, every important building in Athens was a monument that had to be worthy of the ruins of classical antiquity. That meant that it should have the best relationship in space with those monuments and sites of great historical value and the best view towards them, even more so since the ancient monuments were also the stylistic prototypes of the modern ones. That idea was naturally welcomed by everyone, but especially by the enthusiastic architects, archaeologists, and other scholars who got involved in the reconstruction of Athens. In their eyes, that would contribute to the city's glory and to the reconnection of Greece with her ancient past, erasing the recent history of 'barbarism' and 'obscurantism', as they regarded the time of Ottoman domination.

Athens has a particularity, differentiating considerably the context of its urban and architectural evolution from all other European capitals, with the exception of Rome, of course. This particularity is the existence of classical antiquities, which include monuments of supreme artistic value. Until the mid-18th century, when all the routes of the Europeans' grand tour were leading their footsteps to Rome, their acquaintance with antiquity was taking place through the Roman 'filter'. However, after the publication of 'Antiquities of Athens' by the Britons James Stuart and Nicholas Revett in 1762, who were the first to have systematically studied them, the Greek antiquities became for the first time widely known and attracted the interest of European antiquity lovers. That coincided with the publication in 1764 of the German art historian's Johann J. Winckelmann major work, 'Geschichte der Kunst des Alterthums' ('History of Ancient Art'), which supported the novel for that time idea that Greek antiquities were equal in value if not superior to the Roman ones and played a decisive role in their progressive re-evaluation.

Bronze statue of Zeus or Poseidon of Artemision. National Archaeological Museum of Athens, CC0, via Wikimedia Commons

The evolution of that process achieved by the time of the Greek independence led to the conviction that any construction activity in the modern city of Athens, which should result from the medieval town's transformation, could not but take seriously into account the existence, the position, the scale and the state of conservation of those antiquities, depending all new monumental buildings on them.

The above belief found the opportunity to be expressed since December 1834, when Athens became the new capital, replacing the provisional one, Nafplion. That new capital was chosen exactly because of its antiquities, contrary to all practical arguments that would have led the choice to any other city than that one, Athens having the least geographical and financial qualifications to assume that role. Moreover, among several alternative solutions about the exact siting of the new city, the final choice was exactly the one connecting it in space most firmly with its ancient predecessor, against all practical considerations.

The newly appointed King of Greece, who transferred his court to Athens, was Otto, the underage son of King Ludwig I of Bavaria. Otto's father was perhaps the greatest antiquity lover among all European monarchs of his time, as it is suggested by his extensive neoclassical building program in Munich and his rich collections of ancient Greek art. The choice of his son for the Greek throne by the Great Powers had, therefore, as a natural consequence the particularly intense influence of German classicism in Greece. That fact reinforced the decisive role of antiquities in the capital's creation.

The first decades of the independent Greek State are characterized by an intense idealism in every project, which had no connection with the material realities of the country but counted on a very imminent expansion towards all territories inhabited by Greeks and a consequent spectacular change of its conditions. That idealism is also reflected in the first propositions made for the new capital's city plan.

The first official city plan made in 1833 was commissioned by the Greek Government to the Greek architect Stamatios Kleanthes and his German colleague Eduard Schaubert. In it, the modern city's planning demonstrates complete respect for antiquities, although we don't know if that was a request of the Government or if they decided so themselves. In any case, the two architects go as far as proposing the demolition of an important part of the city of Ottoman times, to the advantage of the excavation area, as they mention themselves in their Memorandum. In their plan, all the area between the Acropolis and Hadrian's Library, densely built in pre-revolutionary times, appears unbuilt. As for the street network, it is clearly dependent on antiquities and ancient sites. Therefore, the bisector of the urban triangle, namely Athena Street (Athinas), connects the Royal Palace to the Acropolis and the Ancient Agora. Stadium Street (Stadiou), the right side of the triangle, connects the palace to the ancient stadium, while Piraeus Street (Pireos), the left side, ensures the connection with Athens' homonymous ancient port.

It is noteworthy that, with the exception of the Royal Palace, no other public building lies on the plan's visual axes. Here the antiquities become 'points of view', playing the role held in other capitals by public edifices. The latter keep a clear distance from ancient monuments, although they are substantially larger. Moreover, the two architects' plan lacks completely new monumental constructions like triumphal arcs, etc., which confirms their respect for antiquities. Nevertheless, the plan's intense symmetry makes it clear that the two architects took into consideration neither the ground's inclination towards the southwest nor the concentration of most historic sites in the same direction vis-à-vis the city's historical core.

The German architect Alexander Ferdinand von Quast, who made observations on the Kleanthes and Schaubert project and offered his own proposal, is perhaps the most idealist among the professionals who expressed their opinion on the creation of the modern city. Although he never set his foot in the Greek capital, he took, like many of his countrymen, a vivid interest in what was to his eyes the revival of the most glorious city of all time. Needless to say that he had no idea of the situation in which the object of his admiration was in his time, as it was the case for many of the visionaries who got involved in the creation of modern Athens.

Von Quast thought that the modern city should have developed at some distance from the archaeological zone, along the axis connecting the old city with the port of Piraeus to the southwest of the Acropolis. He writes that the public buildings of the new capital should be concentrated as much as possible in the same place, in order to create an important impression. Therefore, he imagined them at the foot of the Acropolis. He even suggested the creation of a viaduct connecting the Cathedral on the ancient court of the Areopagus with the Acropolis' Propylaia, namely, religious with political power, since the Royal Palace would be built on the Acropolis, according to the project of Carl Friedrich Schinkel. Von Quast put the Cathedral on the Areopagus, where Saint Paul had preached. Like others, he was imagining the cultural institutions on the shore of Ilissus. Naturally, he ignored the lamentable state of the river in his time.

However, the Kleanthes and Schaubert project needed too much money to be realized, because of the expropriations it would mean for the creation of such wide avenues and extended gardens and squares over private land. Therefore, the Bavarian architect Leo von Klenze, official architect of King Ludwig of Bavaria, undertook in 1834 to adapt it to Greek realities. Apart from changing the scale of streets, gardens, and squares to minimize the expropriation cost, he gave the antiquities an even more preponderant place and proposed a town of a size permitting them to prevail everywhere. He also connected the Royal Palace directly with the antiquities and proposed its construction in the area of the ancient cemetery of Kerameikos, one of the most sacred archaeological sites of all Greece. The royal residence would thus have a direct visual relationship to the Acropolis, the ancient parliament of the Pnyx, the Areopagus, and the Royal Garden, including the Theseion (temple of Hephaistos). Von Klenze also relocated the Cathedral and introduced the cultural buildings to their actual location, establishing thus a new hierarchy of God, king, and culture vis-a-vis the Acropolis. He was also the first to introduce in the plan the avenue constituting the central part of the 'monumental axis', known then as the Boulevard, today's University Street (Panepistimiou).

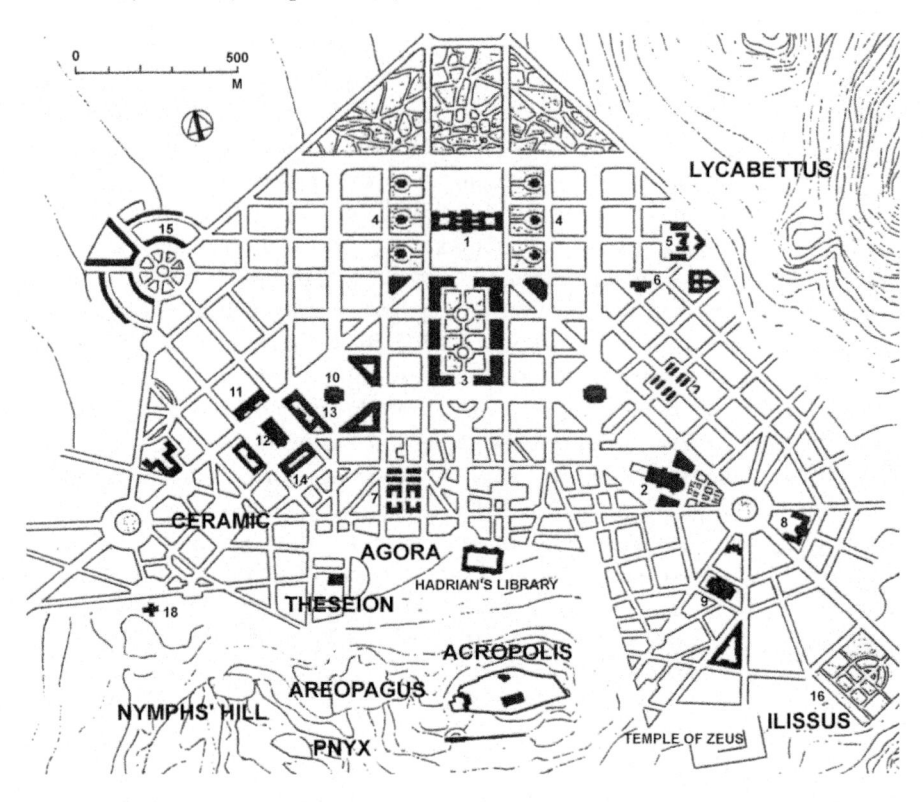

Plan of Stamatios Kleanthes and Eduard Schaubert for the new city of Athens (redrawn by the author, with the addition of location names): 1.Royal Palace 2.Cathedral 3.Central Market 4.Ministries 5.Garrison 6.Mint 7.Market 8.Academy 9.Library 10. Stock Exchange 11.Parliament 12.Church 13.Post Office 14.Headquarters 15.Oil-Press 16.Botanical Garden 17.Exhibition Hall 18.Observatory

It seems that von Klenze's project takes much more into consideration the particularities of the Athenian landscape since the initial plan's symmetry is now adapted to them. Nevertheless, even von Klenze's simpler plan was too expensive to apply, for the same reasons as the previous one.

In consequence, several partial plans modifying parts of his project according to the moment's needs and possibilities had to follow. Contrary to the existence of practical principles too in the first master plan of Kleanthes and Schaubert, the following projects for separate parts of the city reveal an intense desire to locate the important public functions on sites of major archaeological and historical value, without presenting an equal interest in functionality. This is apparent in von Klenze's proposition for the Museum, which he called Pantechneion. He positioned it in 1835 at the same place he had previously proposed for the Royal Palace, at the Kerameikos, next to the temple of Hephaistos (Theseion). The choice of the same place for a building of a totally different destination from the one he himself had initially proposed is very eloquent.

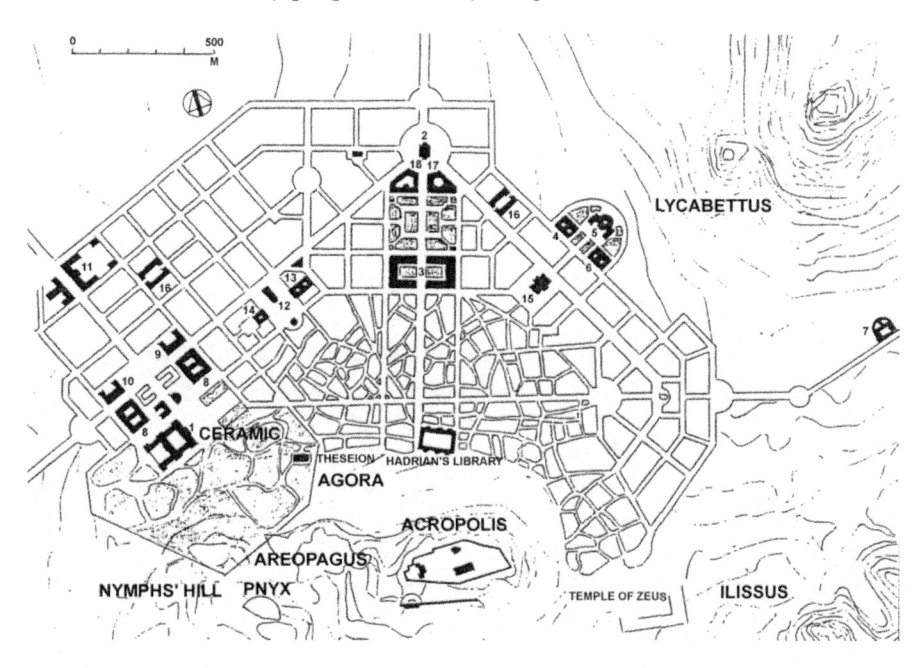

Modification of Kleanthes and Schaubert plan by Leo von Klenze (re-drawn by the author, with the addition of location names): 1.Royal Palace 2.Cathedral 3.Central Market 4.Academy 5.Library 6.University 7.Exhibition Hall 8.Ministries 9.Senate 10.Parliament 11.Camp 12.Church 13.Post Office 14.Prison and Police 15.Theatre 16.Markets 17.Bishop's Palace 18.Schools

The preference for that particular site is impressively insistent. Much later, in 1857, the same area was selected by King Otto and the Government for the construction of the Academy, with enthusiastic remarks about the site's qualities, none of the latter practical, though. Those in favour of that choice sustained that the location was 'prominent' and 'extremely safe'. Others, however, considered as a big sin the construction of modern Athens on the ruins of the ancient city. Moreover, the proximity of the classical monuments would diminish the building's architectural value. Nevertheless, the same place was proposed in 1865 for the construction of the Archaeological Museum. Also, Queen Amalia, King Otto's wife, wanted initially the Royal Garden, created under her supervision, to extend as far as the temple of Hephaistos, in the same area, but she withdrew because of the reactions generated by the existence of antiquities, which would be threatened.

The same issue emerged with the Observatory, which was built on the Nymphs' hill, in spite of the intense objections of the Academy of Munich. As the professor of Athens' University Georgios Vouris mentioned in the speech he made during the Observatory's foundation ceremony, the new building was being built close to the Pnyx, where the famous ancient astronomer Meton had his 'heliotropium'. That reference alone gives us an idea of the emotion caused by such comparisons and, especially, by the pride that no other city in the world could boast of such a privilege. Only this way we can understand the unacceptable for us insistence on building modern monuments next to the ancient ones.

It seems that the ideological – symbolical factor was the only one capable of surmounting the objective difficulties for the materialization of the projects concerning the siting of public buildings, at least those whose function could associate them with famous ancient buildings and therefore bestow upon them intense ideological weight. The most debated case is that of the so-called Athenian Trilogy, not by coincidence, since that complex (University, Academy, Museum at first, and finally National Library) was destined to include the capital's major cultural foundations, which could thus be associated with their equivalent ancient predecessors. The buildings composing that complex were the only ones built at the location predicted by all the city plans, although in a different combination. The selected location was not at all random, since it was –as they thought at that time- next to the ancient Lyceum, the school of Aristotle, close to the Stadium and Ilissus, constituting a direct reference to the historical continuity between ancient and modern Greek civilization. It is only in their case that von Klenze put limits to possible changes of his plans, discouraging the transfer of cultural foundations from the city's eastern part. Additionally, to ensure that the complex would be completed, special construction terms were imposed around it. That means that the only public buildings that maintained their initial location after so many changes and new local plans were exactly the cultural buildings, which kept their connection with the supposed location of one of the most famous cultural institutions of antiquity (which, however, was discovered in 1997 more to the South). That demonstrates perhaps more than anything the force of the ideological factor in the siting of public architecture in the Greek capital.

There were projects predicting the construction of public buildings not just close to the antiquities, but sometimes even above them, with the expected negative consequences. The first and most famous case is that of the aforementioned Schinkel's project. In spite of Schinkel's great knowledge and estimation of classical antiquity, his proposal meant the edification of a huge complex which, in spite of his assurances to the contrary, would eclipse and practically destroy ancient monuments.

However, after the practical difficulties of locating public buildings in archaeological sites were acknowledged, the efforts tended rather towards ensuring them the best view of those sites. In perhaps no other city in the world, the issue of view and orientation of major architectural monuments was put as seriously as in Athens. For 19th century classicists, Greeks and foreigners, Athens was the most privileged city from that point of view, having a natural environment of rare beauty and simultaneously associated with historical and mythological memories unique in the world.

The great diversity of the Athenian landscape, with its multitude of hills, made it extremely sensitive to human interventions. As had been recognized, the hills played the role of pediments or frames for the monuments: the latter, if small, would disappear; if large, they would overwhelm the landscape's elements. Once the uniqueness of the Athenian landscape was realized, the creators of the new capital wanted to enhance it and relate monumental buildings to it.

Since the beginning, the effort to relate the monumental architecture of Athens to its historic landscape became obvious. Naturally, that desire was more intense in the case of the Royal Palace, because of its great symbolical value in a regime of absolute monarchy. The view through the columns of the Parthenon was one of the reasons why von Quast approved Schinkel's bold project.

The German architect Friedrich Stauffert and the German archaeologist Ludwig Ross made similar remarks about the view from the royal residence of the Kleanthes and Schaubert project. From the hill where their palace was located, there would be a view towards the Acropolis, the Areopagus, the Nymphs' hill, the Pnyx, the modern city, Piraeus, the islands of Aegina and Salamis, the Olive Forest where Plato's Academy had been, and the mountains of Parnes, Lycabettus, and Hymettus.

In a similar way, von Klenze writes about the location proposed by his project that no other European capital presented such advantages for siting a royal palace, giving a full description of all interesting views. Moreover, we know that the view played an important role in the selection of the site where the Royal Palace was finally built, in today's Constitution (Syntagma) Square. As has been repeatedly observed, the selected location has the best possible view of all historic sites of the Attica basin, from the Acropolis to Salamis and Aegina (Attica is the district of Athens).

Apart, however, from the Royal Palace, a similar interest in the orientation towards those sites is also observed in the case of other public buildings. The University is clearly oriented to the Acropolis. According to the text accompanying the publication of the plans of the University in 1851, 'the happiest among us are the students of Athens', because of the historic sites they contemplate from the University's Propylaia.

It is obvious that the southwestern orientation was considered to be the best, offering the richest view, as much to the Attica basin as to the Saronic gulf. That was intensified by the ground's inclination towards the bed of Cephisus, the main river of the Attica basin. The siting of the public buildings of Athens shows that that view was aimed at in most cases, contrary to the homogeneity of the Kleanthes and Schaubert project. The Zappeion Exhibition Hall is turned more to the South, probably because the closest antiquities are the ruins of the temple of Zeus, in that direction.

From the above facts, we can see the existence of a very special factor in the process of creation of the modern city of Athens in the 19th century, emanating from the enthusiastic discovery of Greek antiquity some decades earlier. Antiquity lovers saw the creation of the newly installed Greek kingdom's capital as a unique opportunity to revive the object of their visions.

Unfortunately, that wish, arising from the intention to create a glorious capital, had to be put aside by the most prosaic development possible. The new kingdom's desperate financial condition, together with its lack of organization, made the realization of any organized project impossible, the Government having no money to buy the necessary plots. Moreover, the social complications of the expropriations predicted by all the aforementioned projects were too heavy for a State of such limited resources. The result was that the final siting of a very important part of the public buildings of Athens depended often on the availability of land wherever possible, independently of any consideration of view, historical value, or functional advantages.

Nevertheless, the buildings of the 'Monumental Axis', representing the country's rebirth and reminding of its glorious past in the cultural field seemed to escape that rule and follow a different course, based on the idealistic principles set especially for them. More than that, the importance attributed to them managed to replace the initial geometrical form of the new capital's organization, which was based on rational town planning principles, with a different, linear form, satisfying their visual connection to their ancient prototypes. That result is visible even today since those buildings still form the major part of the Greek capital's recent architectural heritage.

24. The 'Great Promenade'
The connection of the archaeological sites of Athens with the modern city

The third itinerary corresponds to what is officially known as the 'Great Promenade'. It is a pedestrian zone linking most of the major archaeological sites of Athens. Although these sites are chronologically anterior to most of the sights presented previously, they are presented last. The reason is that the 'Great Promenade' was created only at the beginning of the 21st century, linking sites that were previously 'lost' in the urban fabric of the modern city and often difficult to find and access. The image they present today is largely the result of these recent interventions, therefore this book recommends this order in their visit. However, if you prefer, you can always follow the 'Great Promenade' and visit these archaeological sites before following the other two proposed itineraries.

When Athens became the capital of Greece, it was a town of only 10,000 people. As we saw previously, in 1833, two architects, Stamatios Kleanthes and Eduard Schaubert, undertook the creation of a plan for a modern city next to the old one. According to that project, a big part of the old town would disappear in order to permit the necessary excavations for the discovery of the ancient city. In that area, a vast archaeological park would be created. But this plan demanded excessive funds for the purchase of the necessary land, so in 1834, Leo von Klenze had to make a new one, limiting the archaeological zone. He also reduced the connection of ancient monuments and archaeological sites with the existing town, preferring a looser relationship between them.

But even that project was applied with modifications limiting furthermore the archaeological zone's surface and practically not connecting the ancient monuments with the modern city. The ancient monuments had to stay hidden between or under other buildings for many years. However, the issue of the connection between the ancient and the modern city remained alive through numerous books, public documents, and articles in newspapers of the time, without being able to become a reality, because of the lack of the enormous funds it needed.

Meanwhile, Athens became bigger and bigger, its population surpassing 4,000,000 people, which made the disappearance of ancient monuments more evident and the realization of the dream of the 19th century more difficult.

However, in 1985 the Master Plan of Athens was voted, elaborating the basic axes of its future development. These included the creation of an Archaeological Park and the amelioration of life quality through the rehabilitation of neglected areas. This Archaeological Park in the centre of the city, a big open museum, includes the most famous ancient and byzantine monuments, the old town and other buildings, squares, axes, and areas of historical character. All the above are linked through the 'Great Promenade'.

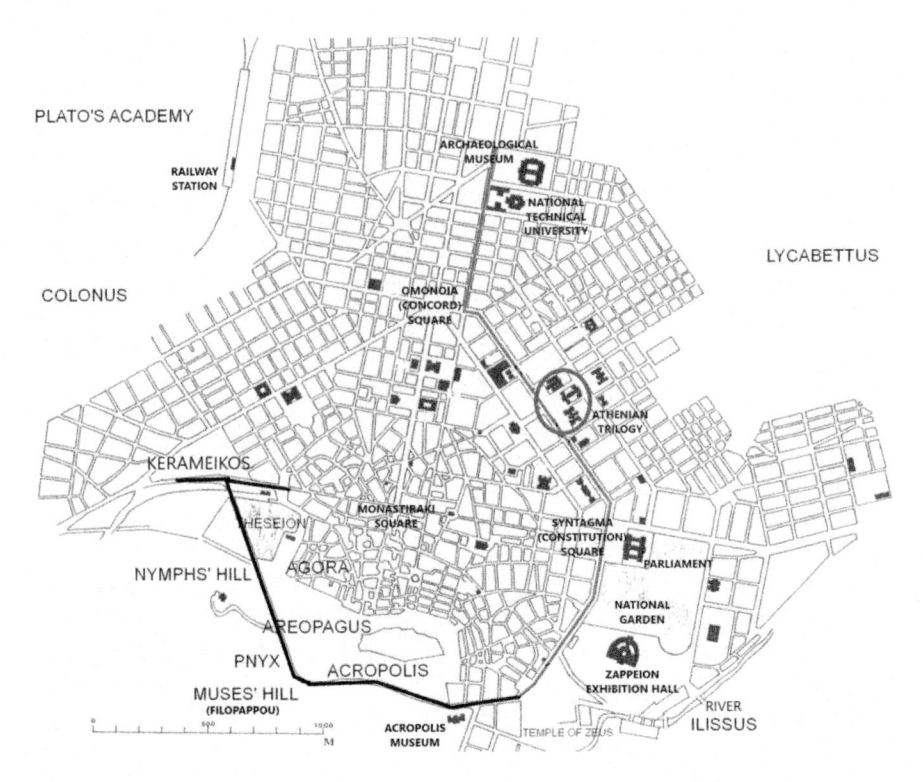

Athens in the 19th century (drawn by the author). Now it is surrounded by a huge built area composing the modern metropolis. The black line on the lower and left part of the plan is the 'Great Promenade', the pedestrian zone created in 2001-2004 to unite the archaeological sites of Athens. All these sites are indicated in regular letters. Sites and buildings of modern Athens are indicated in bold letters. The 'Monumental Axis', indicated by the grey line on the right part of the plan, is the proposed itinerary in case you want to discover the main monuments of neoclassical Athens, the city created as the capital of the newly founded Greek State

The 'Great Promenade' concerns the transformation of Saint Denis (Dionysiou Areopagitou) and Saint Paul (Apostolou Pavlou) avenues into a pedestrian zone, but also a pole of recreation, as it was in ancient times when it lined the cultural buildings, the Odeon of Pericles, the ancient Theatre of Dionysus, and the Roman theatre (Odeon of Herodes Atticus). Open spaces of public use were created, points of reference, vistas to main archaeological sites, etc. This pedestrian zone permits a comfortable visit to the major part of the Archaeological Park.

The soil's relief and the natural itineraries, more or less the same as in ancient times, were enhanced by making vegetation denser or sparser accordingly. On the former Saint Paul Avenue, there is the biggest belvedere to the archaeological sites from the Acropolis to the temple of Hephaistos (Theseion). The major modern attraction on this axis is undoubtedly the new Acropolis Museum, which replaced the obsolete old museum on the hill of the Acropolis.

Our itinerary begins at the same point as the previous one, that of the 'Monumental Axis'. Namely, at the junction of the avenues Amalias and Dionysiou Areopagitou, where the pedestrian zone of the 'Great Promenade' begins.

Just opposite, you will see the Arch of Hadrian and the temple of Zeus. These monuments are isolated from the rest of the zone because of the existence of Amalias Avenue. It is predicted that the portion of the avenue in front of the temple will become underground, permitting pedestrians direct access. Behind the temple (to the southeast) is the only visible part of the second river of Athens, Ilissus, at a beautiful spot, next to the church of Aghia Fotini.

The Arch of Hadrian

The Arch of Hadrian is a monumental gateway resembling a Roman triumphal arch. It spanned an ancient road from the centre of Athens to the complex of structures on the eastern side of the city. It has been proposed that the arch was built to celebrate the adventus (arrival) of the Roman emperor Hadrian and to honour him for his many benefactions to the city, on the occasion of the dedication of the nearby temple of Zeus in 131 or 132 AD. Since Hadrian had become an Athenian citizen nearly two decades before the monument was built, it has been argued that the inscriptions on the arch honour him as an Athenian rather than as the Roman emperor. It is not certain who commissioned the arch, although it is probable that it was the citizens of Athens. There are two inscriptions on the arch, facing in opposite directions, naming both Theseus and Hadrian as founders of Athens. The early idea, however, that the arch marked the line of the ancient city wall, and thus the division between the old and the new quarters of the city, has been shown to be false by further excavation.

The Arch of Hadrian

The temple of Zeus

The temple of Olympian Zeus, also known as the Olympieion or Columns of the Olympian Zeus, is a colossal temple, dedicated to 'Olympian' Zeus, a name originating from his position as head of the Olympian gods. Construction began in the 6th century BC during the rule of the Athenian tyrants, who wanted to build the greatest temple in the world, but it was not completed until the reign of the Roman Emperor Hadrian in the 2nd century AD, some 638 years after the project had begun. During the Roman period, the temple, which included 104 colossal columns, was the largest temple in Greece and housed one of the largest cult statues in the ancient world. The temple's glory was short-lived, as it fell into disuse after being pillaged during the barbarian invasion of the Heruli in 267 AD, just about a century after its completion. It was probably never repaired and was reduced to ruins thereafter. In the centuries after the end of the ancient world, it was used as a quarry for building materials. Despite that, a substantial part of the temple remains today, notably sixteen of the original colossal columns.

The temple of Zeus

The ancient Stadium (Kallimarmaro)

The project of the 'Great Promenade' also includes a future connection with the ancient Stadium, where the first modern Olympic Games of 1896 took place after it was restored. You will find it if you follow Olgas Avenue, between the temple of Zeus and the Zappeion Exhibition Hall.

The ancient Stadium, where the Olympic Games of 1896 took place after it was restored. Photo by RzlBrz007700 (pixabay.com), public domain work

The new Acropolis Museum. It contains artefacts exclusively from the Acropolis, including the sculptures of the temples that escaped the pillage of Lord Elgin

The northern and southern slopes of the Acropolis

This part of the 'Great Promenade' concerns the connection of the slopes of the Acropolis with the other sites and the highlighting of the numerous not very well known ancient monuments lying there. It also includes the arrangement of the areas of two major monuments, the Roman Odeon of Herodes Atticus and especially the ancient Theatre of Dionysus.

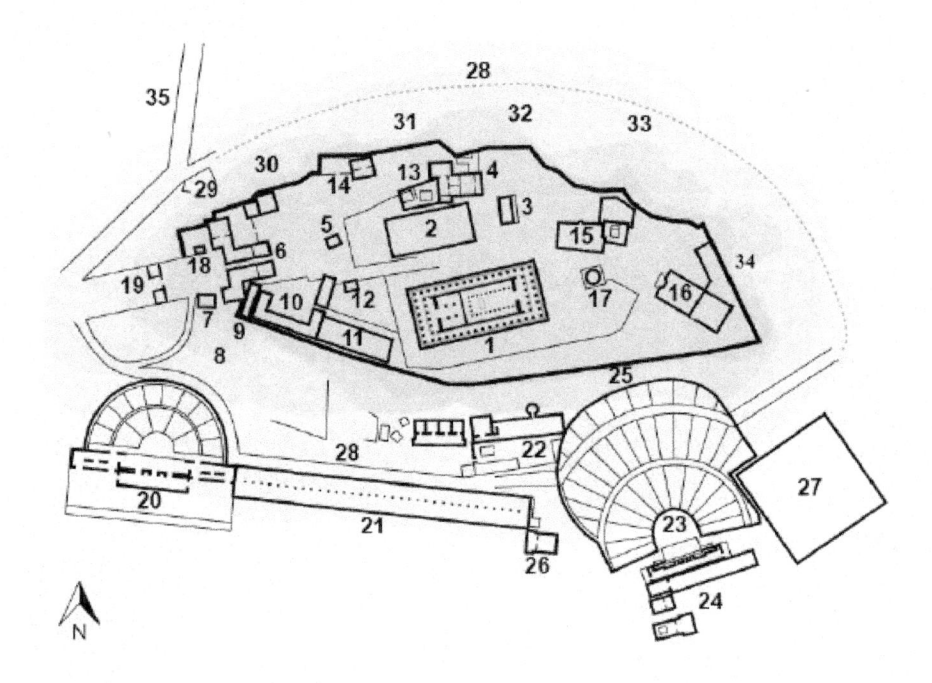

The Acropolis of Athens and its surroundings. Source: Tomisti, CC BY-SA 4.0 <https://creativecommons.org/licenses/by-sa/4.0>, via Wikimedia Commons

1.Parthenon 2.Temple of Athena Polias 3.Altar of Athena Polias 4.Erechtheion 5.Statue of Athena Promachos 6.Propylaia 7.Temple of Athena Nike 8.Sanctuary of Aphrodite Pandemos and Peitho 9.Pelasgian wall (Mycenaean wall) 10.Sanctuary of Artemis Brauronia 11.Chalkotheke 12.Sanctuary of Athena Ergane (possible location) 13.Pandroseion 14.Arrhephoreion 15.Sanctuary of Zeus Polieus 16.Sanctuary of Pandion 17.Temple of Augustus and Roma 18.Memorial of Agrippa 19.Beulé Gate 20.Odeon of Herodes Atticus 21.Stoa of Eumenes 22.Asclepieion 23.Theatre of Dionysus 24.Sanctuary of Dionysus Eleuthereus 25.Choragic Monument of Thrasyllos 26.Choragic Monument of Nicias 27.Odeon of Pericles 28.Peripatos 29.Klepsydra 30.Caves of Apollo Hypoakraios, Olympian Zeus, and Pan 31.Mycenaean fountain 32.Sanctuary of Aphrodite and Eros 33.Peripatos inscription 34.Aglaureion 35.Panathenaic Way

The Theatre of Dionysus

If you follow the 'Great Promenade' from the Arch of Hadrian to the West, the first site you will encounter on your right is that of the ancient Theatre of Dionysus. It is considered the first theatre in the world, the cradle of ancient Greek tragedy and comedy. It owes its name to Dionysus, god of wine. The great Dionysian celebrations were held there every year in his honour. They were initially ritual songs, dances, and ritual sacrifices resulting in theatrical performances. This is where the famous classical tragedies of Aeschylus, Sophocles, and Euripides were created. The theatre dates back to the 5th century BC. In the beginning, it consisted of just a beaten earth orchestra and a stage built in wood, and the spectators took their places on the natural slope of the site. Around 420 BC wooden tiers were built. The stone construction we see today, where the stone steps replaced those of wood, was created under Lycurgus between 338 and 326 BC. The theatre had 78 rows of seats and could hold 17,000 spectators. The first row of seats (proedria) was made up of 67 marble seats with backs, reserved for the various dignitaries, magistrates, people of distinction, competition referees. The koilon (the spectators' space) is arranged in a hemicycle around the orchestra, where the dancing and singing of the choir took place. In the middle of the orchestra, there was an altar, on which the victims were presented to the gods. The actors moved on the proskenion, in front of the stage building.

The Theatre of Dionysus. Photo by Jebulon, CC0, via Wikimedia Commons

The Asclepieion

Immediately west of the theatre, you can visit the sanctuary of Asclepius or Asclepieion. Dedicated to Asclepius, god of medicine whose cult was imported from Epidaurus to Athens after 420 BC, the sanctuary's purpose was the healing of the sick. It has a square fence, a temple, and a portico (stoa) of Doric order, consisting of a double gallery separated by a row of columns, built in the 4th century BC. Subsequently, the core of the Asclepieion (stoa and temple) was integrated into an early Christian basilica. The portico included a cave, later converted into a Christian chapel, with a source still considered to be curative. Restoration work was carried out in the 2010s, to make the remains clearer to the visitor.

Neoclassical architecture along the 'Great Promenade', opposite the Acropolis

The Odeon of Herodes Atticus

West of the Asclepieion, there is the Odeon of Herodes Atticus, dominating the western end on the southern slope of the Acropolis. It was the third odeon constructed in ancient Athens after the Odeon of Pericles on the southern slope (5th century BC) and the Odeon of Agrippa in the Ancient Agora (15 BC). The construction of the monument during the 2nd century AD was sponsored by Tiberius Claudius Herodes Atticus, a renowned member of an important Athenian family and a benefactor. He did this in remembrance of his wife Regilla, who died in 160 AD. The exact date of construction is unknown, but it was certainly built sometime after Regilla's death and 174 AD when the traveller and geographer Pausanias visited Athens and referred to the monument in great admiration.

The roofed odeon served mainly musical festivals and could host up to 5,000 spectators. Both wall surfaces were covered by poros stone blocks, while the interior was filled with quarry-faced stones. The semi-circular cavea (in Greek koilon, auditorium) was hewn out of the rock. It was divided into two sections by a corridor; each section included 32 rows of seats made of white marble. The upper corridor of the cavea was probably bordered by a gallery. The semi-circular orchestra was paved with white marble. The scene was raised and the scenic wall extended over three levels. Arched openings decorated the wall's upper part, while the lower part contained several three-columned projecting porticos and niches for the placement of statues, characteristic of Roman theatres. The scene was flanked by staircases leading to the upper section. A gallery lined the front of the outer scenic wall. Mosaic floors with geometrical and linear patterns covered the entrances to the staircases. The monument was an extremely expensive construction, which is also confirmed by ancient testimonies referring mostly to the cedar wood used for the roof. It seems that the roof of the cavea, with a 38m radius, had no internal pillars since there are no traces of such pillars, which constitutes a unique construction achievement even in our days. To the East, the odeon was connected to the stoa (portico) of Eumenes, built about three centuries earlier (197-159 BC), by Eumenes, king of Pergamon, to offer to the spectators of the Theatre of Dionysus protection from sun and rain.

The odeon was destroyed in 267 AD at the incursion of the Heruli and was never reconstructed. Later, it was incorporated within the city's fortifications. Its southern wall became part of the later Roman wall erected in the 3rd century AD, whereas in the 13th century the high scenic wall was included in the wall surrounding the base of the Acropolis hill. In the 14th century, the embankments covering the lower part of the monument's southern wall were so thick, that the entrances were no longer visible. The monument was restored in 1952-1953 with marble from the Dionysos area, similar to the original Pentelic marble. Since 1957, it houses art festivals (concerts, ancient drama performances, etc.) mostly as part of the Athens Festival.

The Odeon of Herodes Atticus. In the background, on the right, is the monument of Philopappos atop the Muses hill. Photo by Mstyslav Chernov, CC BY-SA 3.0 <https://creativecommons.org/licenses/by-sa/3.0>, via Wikimedia Commons

The Acropolis

The Acropolis. In the foreground, on the left, is the Odeon of Herodes Atticus. Photo by Christophe Meneboeuf, CC BY-SA 3.0 <https://creativecommons.org/licenses/by-sa/3.0>, via Wikimedia Commons

The Propylaia of the Acropolis. Photo by Paolo Villa, CC BY-SA 4.0 <https://creativecommons.org/licenses/by-sa/4.0>, via Wikimedia Commons

Temple of Athena Nike, on the right of the Propylaia. Photo by Jebulon, CC0, via Wikimedia Commons

The Parthenon. Photo by Steve Swayne, CC BY 2.0 <https://creativecommons.org/licenses/by/2.0>, via Wikimedia Commons

Sculptures from the east pediment of the Parthenon, now in the British Museum. Photo by Andrew Dunn, via Wikimedia Commons

Metopes of the Parthenon with Centauromachy, now in the British Museum. Photo by Carole Raddato from FRANKFURT, Germany, CC BY-SA 2.0 <https://creativecommons.org/licenses/by-sa/2.0>, via Wikimedia Commons

The Erechtheion. Photo by Jebulon, CC0, via Wikimedia Commons

The Caryatids of the Erechtheion, public domain work

The 'Great Promenade' is dominated by the Acropolis, the most important site in Athens and in the whole of Greece. It is an ancient citadel located on a rocky outcrop above the city rising 150 m above sea level and contains the remains of several ancient buildings of great architectural and historical significance. You will find access to it on the 'Great Promenade', after the Odeon of Herodes, always on your right.

The word acropolis derives from the Greek words ἄκρον (akron, 'highest point, extremity') and πόλις (polis, 'city'). The term is generic and there are many other acropoleis in Greece.

While the earliest artefacts date to the Middle Neolithic era and there is evidence that the hill was inhabited as far back as the 4th millennium BC, it was Pericles (c. 495–429 BC) in the 5th century BC who coordinated the construction of the buildings whose present remains are the site's most important ones, including the Parthenon, the Propylaia, the Erechtheion and the temple of Athena Nike.

It is certain that a Mycenaean palace stood upon the hill during the late Bronze Age, although it has left no traces. Soon after the palace's construction, a Cyclopean massive circuit wall was built, 760 metres long, up to 10 metres high, and ranging from 3.5 to 6 metres thick. This wall would be the main defence of the Acropolis until the 5th century BC.

We don't know much about how the Acropolis looked like before the Archaic era. A temple to Athena Polias, the tutelary deity of the city, was erected between 570 and 550 BC, at the place where the Parthenon stands today. This Doric limestone building, from which many ruins survive, is referred to as the Hekatompedon (Greek for 'hundred–footed', referring to its length). It is not known if this temple replaced an older one, or just a sacred precinct or altar.

Between 529 and 520 BC, yet another temple was built by the Peisistratids, the tyrants of Athens: the Ancient Temple of Athena. This temple of Athena Polias was built between the Erechtheion and the still-standing Parthenon. The Ancient Temple was destroyed along with the whole city during the Second Persian invasion of Greece in 480–479 BC; however, the temple was probably reconstructed in 454 BC, since the treasury of the Delian League was transferred in it. The temple may have been burnt down during 406/405 BC as Xenophon mentions that the old temple of Athena was set afire.

Around 500 BC the Hekatompedon was dismantled to make place for a new grander building, the 'Older Parthenon' (often referred to as the Pre-Parthenon, or 'early Parthenon'). In 485 BC, construction stalled to save resources as Xerxes became king of Persia and war seemed imminent.

The Older Parthenon was still under construction when the Persians invaded and destroyed the city in 480 BC. The building was burned and looted, along with the Ancient Temple and everything else on the rock.

After the end of the Persian Wars, the Athenians incorporated many architectural parts of the unfinished temple (unfluted column drums, triglyphs, metopes, etc.) into the newly built northern curtain wall of the Acropolis, where they served as a prominent 'war memorial' and can still be seen today from Plaka and Monastiraki. The devastated site was cleared of debris. Statuary, cult objects, religious offerings, and architectural members were buried ceremoniously in several deeply dug pits on the hill, serving as a fill for the artificial plateau created around the classic Parthenon. This 'Persian debris' was excavated on the Acropolis by 1890 and gave us among other findings the famous Archaic female statues of the Korai, which we can see in the Acropolis Museum.

Most of the major temples, including the Parthenon, were rebuilt by order of Pericles during the so-called Golden Age of Athens (460–430 BC). Phidias, an Athenian sculptor, and Ictinus and Callicrates, two famous architects, were responsible for the reconstruction.

The Parthenon is a double peripteral Doric temple with several unique and innovative architectural features. The temple proper is divided into pronaos, cella, and opisthodomos, with a separate room at the western end, and is surrounded by a pteron (colonnade) with eight columns on each of the short sides and seventeen columns on the long ones. The interior demonstrates an innovative approach to both new and old elements: inside the cella, a double U-shaped colonnade established a background for the gold and ivory statue of Athena Parthenos, which showed the goddess in full armour carrying Nike (Victory) to the Athenians in her right hand. The western room, where the city's treasures were kept, had four Ionic columns. The two-sloped wooden roof had marble tiles, marble palmette-shaped false antefixes along the edge of its long sides, and false spouts in the shape of lion heads at the corners. Marble statues adorned the corners of the pediments and large, ornate palmettes their apex. The pediments were decorated with sculptural compositions inspired by the life of the goddess Athena. The eastern pediment depicted the birth of the goddess, who sprang from the head of her father, Zeus, before an assembly of the Olympian gods, while the western pediment showed Athena and Poseidon disputing for the possession of the city of Athens before the gods, heroes, and mythical kings of Attica. Ninety-two metopes alternating with triglyphs were placed above the epistyle of the outer colonnade and under the architrave. All of them were adorned with reliefs. Their themes derived from legendary battles: the Gigantomachy was depicted on the eastern side, the Trojan War on the northern side, the Amazonomachy on the western side, and the Centauromachy on the southern side. The frieze, an element of the Ionic order, brilliantly added to this Doric temple along the top of the cella, pronaos, and opisthodomos, depicted the splendid procession of the Panathenaia, the greatest festival of Athens in honour of Athena.

In 437 BC, Mnesicles started building the Propylaia, a monumental gate at the western end of the Acropolis with Doric columns of Pentelic marble, built partly upon the old propylaia of Peisistratos, the tyrant of the 6th century BC. The complex was almost finished in 432 BC and had two wings, the northern one decorated with paintings by Polygnotus, one of the most famous painters of ancient Greece.

About the same time, south of the Propylaia, building started on the small Ionic temple of Athena Nike in Pentelic marble. The temple was finished between 421 BC and 409 BC. It is a small Ionic structure with four monolithic columns on either short side. Above the epistyle, a frieze by sculptor Agorakritos depicted battle scenes between the Greeks and Persians on three sides and, on the eastern side, an assembly of the Olympian gods watching these battles. Little is preserved of the pediments, which are believed to have depicted a Gigantomachy on the western side and an Amazonomachy on the eastern side. Outside the temple, to the East, was the altar. A marble parapet was built in 409 BC along the edge of the bastion for safety reasons. It consists of relief slabs, one metre high, representing winged Victories leading bulls to be sacrificed or sacrificing them or decorating trophies before the seated Athena. Several slabs and parts of the frieze can be seen in the Acropolis Museum; other parts of the frieze were taken by Lord Elgin and are in the British Museum.

Construction of the elegant temple of Erechtheion (421–406 BC) followed a complex plan taking account of the extremely uneven ground and the desire to include several older shrines that existed in the area. The temple was made of Pentelic marble, the frieze of Eleusinian grey stone with white relief figures attached to it, and the foundations of Piraeus stone. The entrance, facing East, is lined with six Ionic columns. The eastern part of the temple was dedicated to Athena Polias and housed the cult statue of Athena, made of olive wood, which the Arrhephoroi draped with the sacred peplos during the Panathenaic festival. The western part, serving the cult of the archaic king Poseidon-Erechtheus, housed the altars of Hephaistos and Voutos, brother of Erechtheus. Little is known about the original plan of the interior which was destroyed by fire in the 1st century BC and has been rebuilt several times. Unusually, the temple has two porches, one on the northwest corner supported by Ionic columns, the other, to the southwest, borne by huge female figures or Caryatids. Created by Alkamenes or Kallimachos, the statues were later named Caryatids after the young women from Karyai of Lakonia who danced in honour of the goddess Artemis. Five of them are in the Acropolis Museum and another in the British Museum, while those on the building are casts. The frieze probably depicted scenes related to the mythical kings of Athens. In the early 19th century, Lord Elgin removed one of the Caryatids and a column and during the Greek War of Independence, the building was bombarded and severely damaged.

Between the temple of Athena Nike and the Parthenon, there was the sanctuary of Artemis Brauronia (or the Brauroneion). The goddess was represented as a bear and worshipped in Brauron, a little town included in the State of Athens. According to Pausanias, a wooden statue of the goddess and a statue of Artemis made by Praxiteles in the 4th century BC co-existed in the sanctuary.

Behind the Propylaia, there was Phidias' gigantic bronze statue of Athena Promachos ('Athena who fights in the front line'), created between 450 BC and 448 BC. The base was 1.50 metres high, while the total height of the statue was 9 metres. The goddess held a lance, the gilt tip of which could be seen as a reflection by crews on ships rounding Cape Sounion, and a giant shield on the left side.

Other monuments that have left almost nothing visible to the present day are the Chalkotheke, the Pandroseion, Pandion's sanctuary, Athena's altar, Zeus Polieus' sanctuary, and, from Roman times, the circular temple of Augustus and Rome.

During the Hellenistic and Roman periods, many of the existing buildings in the area of the Acropolis were repaired, due to damage from age and, occasionally, fire. Monuments to foreign kings were erected, notably those of the kings of Pergamon Attalos II (in front of the north-western corner of the Parthenon), and Eumenes II, in front of the Propylaia. These were rededicated during the early Roman Empire to Augustus or Claudius (it is uncertain which), and Agrippa, respectively. Eumenes sponsored the construction of the aforementioned stoa (portico) on the southern slope. During the Julio-Claudian period, the temple of Rome and Augustus, a small, round edifice, about 23 meters east of the Parthenon, was to be the last significant ancient construction on the summit of the rock.

During the 3rd century AD, under threat from a Herulian invasion, repairs were made to the Acropolis walls, and the 'Beulé Gate' was constructed to restrict entrance in front of the Propylaia, thus re-giving to the Acropolis its ancient use as a fortress.

During the Byzantine period, the Parthenon was used as a church, dedicated to the Virgin Mary. Under the Latin Duchy of Athens (1204-1456), created after the conquest of the Byzantine Empire by the crusaders of the 4th Crusade, the Acropolis functioned as the city's administrative centre, with the Parthenon as its cathedral, and the Propylaia as part of the Ducal Palace. A large tower was added, demolished in the 19th century. After the Ottoman conquest of Athens in 1456, the Parthenon was used as the garrison headquarters of the Turkish army, and the Erechtheion was turned into the governor's private harem. The buildings of the Acropolis suffered significant damage during the 1687 siege by the Venetians. The Parthenon, which was being used as a gunpowder magazine, was hit by artillery shot and damaged severely. Further serious damage was caused in the early 19th century by Lord Elgin, who looted much of the temple's sculptural decoration and sold it to the British Museum.

During subsequent years, the Acropolis was a site of bustling human activity with many Byzantine, Frankish, and Ottoman structures. The dominant feature during the Ottoman period was a mosque inside the now destroyed Parthenon, complete with a minaret.

The Acropolis was besieged thrice during the Greek War of Independence (two sieges from the Greeks in 1821–1822 and one from the Ottomans in 1826–1827). After independence, most constructions dating from the Byzantine, Frankish, and Ottoman periods were cleared from the site in an attempt to restore the monument to its original form, 'cleansed' of all later additions, according to that time's universal restoration principles.

The Acropolis Restoration Project began in 1975 with the goal to reverse the decay of centuries of attrition, pollution, destruction from military actions, and misguided past restorations. The project included collection and identification of all stone fragments from the Acropolis and its slopes and the present philosophy is to restore as much as possible using reassembled original material, with new marble from Mount Pentelicus used sparingly. All restoration is made using titanium dowels and is designed to be completely reversible, in case future experts decide to make changes. A combination of cutting-edge modern technology and extensive research and reinvention of ancient techniques was used. If you visit the Acropolis on a working day, you will see specialized stonemasons working on the monuments with a skill equal to that of their ancient colleagues.

The Areopagus

Opposite the entrance to the Acropolis is the Areopagus hill, a sacred place related to Ares and the chthonic (underworld) deities of punishment and vengeance, also called 'Erinyes' (Furies). It was the place of assembly of the political and judicial body of Areopagus. On the northern edge of the hill, there are the remains of four luxurious houses of the 4th-6th century AD, the so-called 'philosophical schools', which possibly belonged to sophists. South of Areopagus lies a residential district of the ancient municipality of Kollytos. You can see ruins of houses with mosaics on your right if you continue along the 'Great Promenade' after you leave the Acropolis.

The archaeological site of Philopappou

After the access to the Acropolis, always on the 'Great Promenade', on the left, is the free access to the archaeological site of Philopappou. This site includes three important hills of ancient Athens: the Muses hill (or Philopappou), the Nymphs hill, and the Pnyx. It also includes more recent monuments, like the Observatory, atop the Nymphs hill, designed by Theophil Hansen, and the very picturesque church of Saint Demetrius Loumbardiaris. The area also includes a lot of urban greenery. The accesses and itineraries within these sites were the major part of the intervention during the creation of the 'Great Promenade'.

The monument of Philopappos, atop the Muses hill, dates from 114-116 AD. It was erected by the Athenians in honour of the great benefactor of their city, the exiled prince of Commagene, Julius Antiochus Philopappos who settled in Athens, became a citizen and assumed civic and religious offices.

The monument is built of white Pentelic marble on a socle made of poros stone and veneered with slabs of Hymettian marble (from Mount Hymettus, which closes the basin of Athens from the East). The northern side of the monument, which is visible from the Acropolis, was the facade and was adorned with lavish architectural decoration. The central figure is Philopappos, son of Epiphanes, on the left is Antiochus, son of King Antiochus, and on the right was King Seleucus Nicator, son of Antiochus.

Recent investigation has certified that architectural parts of the monument had been used for the construction of the minaret in the Parthenon when the Ottomans transformed the temple into a mosque.

The Pnyx

After leaving the main pedestrian zone towards the access to the hill of the Muses or Philopappou, if you turn right, you will find your way to the Pnyx, the place where the Assembly of the Athenians held its meetings.

The remains found have shown that the Pnyx had three main building periods. In the first period, the natural hillside was used as the auditorium. The surface was evened off by quarrying out the hard limestone, while a straight retaining wall was built on the northern side. In the second period, the arrangement of the auditorium was very different; a high, semi-circular retaining wall was built to the North, supporting an embankment sloping down to the South, namely, in the opposite direction to that of the first period. This was allegedly done in order to make the members of the assembly turn their back to the Acropolis and concentrate on the orator instead of being distracted by the intense construction activity taking place up there after the Persian Wars. The access was ensured by two stairways.

The Pnyx of the third period had exactly the same plan but on a larger scale; the great retaining wall was constructed of large stone blocks quarried from the area, while the new bema was arranged to the South.

The 'Great Promenade' at the quarter of Theseion

Transformation of the lower part of Hermes Street into a pedestrian zone

After the Pnyx and the hill of Philopappos, you will continue on the 'Great Promenade' and reach the quarter of Theseion. At the Byzantine church of Aghioi Asomatoi (the Archangels), the pedestrian zone is divided into two branches: the western one (left) is the pedestrianized lower part of Hermes (Ermou) Street leading to the ancient cemetery of the Kerameikos and the quarter of Gazi; the eastern branch (right) is the equally pedestrianized Hadrian (Adrianou) Street, leading to the Ancient Agora and to Monastiraki.

Hermes (Ermou) Street was one of the first streets created for the modern city of Athens and one of the main axes of the plan made in 1833 by Kleanthes and Schaubert (forming the basis of the urban plan's main triangle), also kept in the plan of Leo von Klenze. The upper (eastern) part of the street, concentrating up to today the retail commerce, recreation, and public services, is a pedestrian zone since 1996; on the contrary, the lower (western) part was connected to industrial activities since the 19th century and was presenting an image of abandonment. The presence of heavy traffic didn't permit the visitor to understand that along this part of the street, there was the very important archaeological site of the ancient cemetery of the Kerameikos. The intervention to that part of Hermes Street permitted the highlighting of the archaeological site and to connect it with the other sites and the rest of the city. At the end of the street is the old Gas Factory (Gazi), nowadays Cultural Centre of the Municipality of Athens next to the very animated quarter of Gazi, one of the epicentres of Athenian nightlife.

The Byzantine church of Aghioi Asomatoi (the Archangels, 11th century)

The ancient cemetery of the Kerameikos and Kerameikos Square

The pedestrianized lower part of Hermes Street leads to Kerameikos Square, a new square created in the place of the shacks of a market. It is the end of the 'Great Promenade' and the nucleus of a new pole in the historical centre of Athens, larger even than Constitution Square (Syntagma), the capital's main square. It was created as the third (southwestern) square of the plan of 1833, which was not completed then, because of the transfer of the Royal Palace from the top of the triangle of the city's plan to the eastern angle (Constitution Square). That unsettled the plan's balance and upgraded excessively the eastern part of the city, leading the western part to decline.

The intervention also included the highlighting of the archaeological site of the ancient cemetery of the Kerameikos, which is accessible from Ermou Street. This is a small part of the ancient Attic demos (meaning community, where the word democracy comes from) of Kerameon, one of the largest demes of ancient Athens, located on the north-western edge of the city. As suggested by its name, the Kerameikos (from the Greek word for pottery) was a settlement of potters and vase painters, and the main production centre of the famous Attic vases. Those parts of the Kerameikos that were located near the riverbank suffered continuously from the overflowing small river Eridanos, and so the area was converted into a burial ground, which gradually developed into the most important cemetery of ancient Athens.

Potters were drawn to the Kerameikos by the clay deposits of the Eridanos, which runs through the archaeological site. The river lay buried for centuries under eight or nine meters of landfill but was uncovered again in the 1960s during archaeological excavations.

The earliest tombs at the Kerameikos date from the Early Bronze Age (2700-2000 BC), and the cemetery appears to have continuously expanded from the sub-Mycenaean period (1100-1000 BC). During the Geometric (1000-700 BC) and Archaic periods (700-480 BC), the number of tombs increased; they were arranged inside tumuli or marked by funerary monuments. The cemetery was used incessantly from the Hellenistic period until the Early Christian period (338 BC until approximately the 6th century AD).

The most important Athenian vases come from the tombs of the Kerameikos. Among them is the famous 'Dipylon Oinochoe', which bears the earliest inscription written in the Greek alphabet (second half of the 8th century BC). The site's small museum houses the finds from the Kerameikos excavations.

Kerameikos. Above, the best-preserved part of the ancient walls of Athens. Next to them are the ruins of the Pompeion, where the preparations for the Panathenaic procession (depicted on the frieze of the Parthenon) took place. Below, funerary monuments, among which that of Hegeso (first from the left)

The Themistoclean wall was built hastily in 478 BC, after the Persian retreat, in order to protect the city from the Spartan threat. It surrounded the entire ancient city of Athens and divided the Kerameikos into two sections, inner and outer Kerameikos. Inner Kerameikos (inside the city walls) developed into a residential neighbourhood, whereas outer Kerameikos remained a cemetery. The section of the wall that crossed the Kerameikos from North to South is preserved to this day, together with two important gates, the Dipylon, the largest and most formal Athenian gate, and the Sacred Gate.

Two important ways, the Demosion Sema, which led to Plato's Academy, and the Sacred Way (Iera Odos), which connected Athens with Eleusis, began at the Dipylon and Sacred Gate (Iera Pyli) respectively. The Sacred Gate was the starting point for the procession of the Eleusinian Mysteries, and the Dipylon was the starting point of the Panathenaic procession, which moved along the Panathenaic Way towards the Acropolis. The preparations for the Panathenaic procession took place inside the Pompeion (pompé meaning procession), a large building (end of the 5th century BC) with a court surrounded by a colonnade, located directly behind the wall, next to the Dipylon.

During the Classical period (5th-4th centuries BC) the streets were lined with cemeteries and funerary monuments, mostly of families, and often decorated with reliefs. Some of the best-known funerary monuments are the tomb of Dexileo, the stele (tombstone) of Hegeso (c. 400 BC), the relief of Demetria and Pamphile, and the marble bull from the funerary enclosure of Dionysios of Kollytos (c. 345 BC).

Outside the Dipylon, along the street leading to Plato's Academy, lay the Demosion Sema, or Public Cemetery, the burial place of Athenian notables and war heroes. This is where Pericles delivered his famous Funeral Oration (Epitaphios) for those who died during the first year of the Peloponnesian War (430 BC).

Here are some excerpts from an article written by the archaeologist Semni Karouzou on the most famous funerary sculpture of the Kerameikos, that you will find nowhere else. I chose it because I believe it gives a very good idea of the spirit of the whole ancient Greek sculpture:

'Who was this young woman of unspeakable nobility of countenance and stature who was praised by art and respected by time? We know nothing more about her than the inscription in beautiful, simple classic letters: Hegeso of Proxenos. It seems more likely that she was the daughter of Proxenos and that she was buried in her husband's family grave. It is the noblest Attic tombstone. The Attic tombstones, even the most 'manual' ones, have a deep, discreetly tragic humanity, unprecedented at the time in the world. The best ones are real works of art because they were made by great craftsmen.'

Funerary monument of Hegeso. National Archaeological Museum of Athens, CC BY-SA 3.0 <http://creativecommons.org/licenses/by-sa/3.0/>, via Wikimedia Commons

'The sculptor of Hegeso (N.B. probably Callimachus) gave us such a wonderful creation. In her face, in her movements, he did not show any complaints, no protests. She moves us because we see her stately, light, and beautiful, sitting comfortably on the elegant chair holding in her fingers -on these melodic fingers- a necklace. This hand, the most Attic of the female hands of the funerary steles, concentrates the eyes of the figures as it is located in the centre of the composition. The sculptor did not want the image to be burdened with more figures; only the young slave, who holds the box of jewels -as was really the case in the house that Hegeso once brightened- is standing in front of her mistress.'

'Hegeso is free, elevated above every individual feature, as a symbolic image of transient but heroized youth. Classical art refused to represent the dead defeated by 'pernicious' death; it only indicated it by representing the good aspect of life, which is so short; in contrast to the classicist art of the 19th century, where we find the extinction of the young dead by the means of death.'

'Only in Athens, the city of ancient history and so much nobility could such an image be created. What did it matter that a Spartan general had demolished its well-built walls a few years before? It remained the first, the master in the spirit and in the art that annihilated death and offered it eternal life.' (N.B. the stele of Hegeso was created just a few years after Athens was defeated by Sparta in the Peloponnesian War).

Transformation of Hadrian Street into a pedestrian zone

To continue on the 'Great Promenade', you have to come back to the church of Aghioi Asomatoi and take the eastern (right) branch of the pedestrian zone. This is Hadrian (Adrianou) Street, one of the oldest and most historical streets of Athens. A part of it has a very particular place in the city since it lies between the built area and the archaeological sites. It has commercial and recreational use, one of the gates to the Ancient Agora, and a very wide view of the Acropolis. Here, the main interventions were the exclusion of vehicles and the restoration of the neoclassical houses on one side of it (the other side is lined by the Ancient Agora).

The Ancient Agora

From this part of Adrianou Street, you can enter the Ancient Agora.

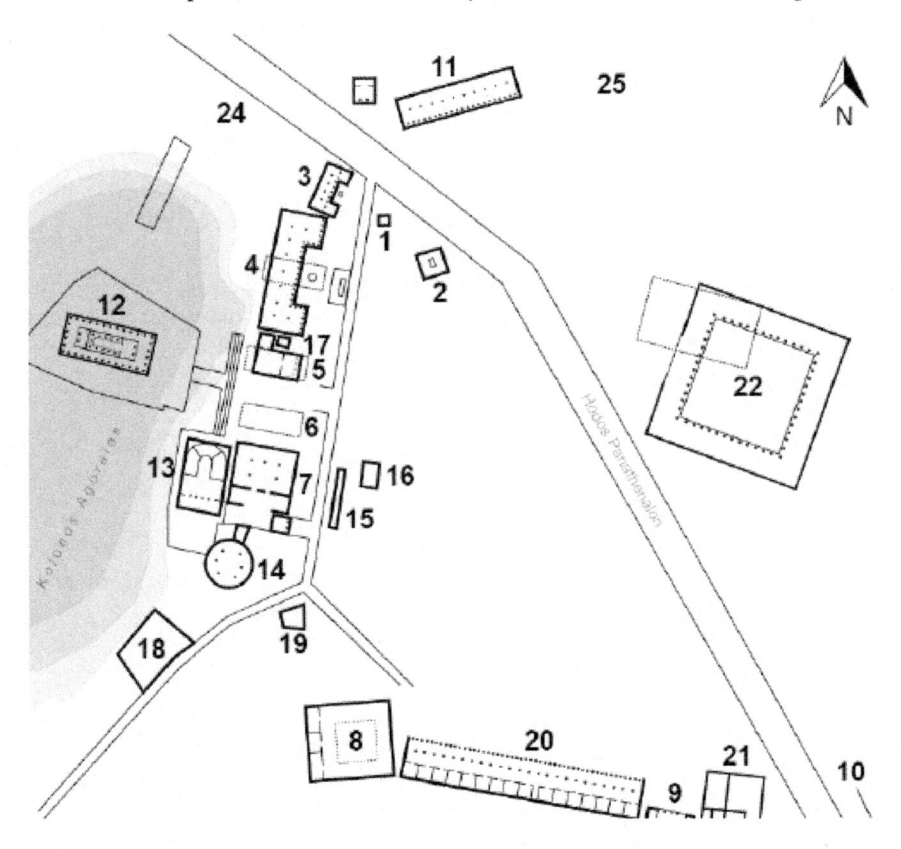

Plan of the Agora of Athens during the Classical period. Source: Tomisti, CC BY-SA 4.0 <https://creativecommons.org/licenses/by-sa/4.0>, via Wikimedia Commons

1.Leokoreion 2.Altar of Twelve Gods 3.Royal Stoa (Stoa Basileios) 4.Temple of Zeus, later Stoa of Zeus 5.Old and new temple of Apollo Patroos 6.Old Metroon 7.Bouleuterion 8.Aiakeion (not Heliaia as previously thought) 9.Southeast Fountain House (often Enneakrunos) 10.Eleusinion (outside the map) 11.Stoa Poikile 12.Temple of Hephaistos 13.New Bouleuterion 14.Prytanikon, later Tholos 15.Monument of Eponymous Heros 16.Altar of Zeus Agoraios 17.Temple of Zeus Phratrios and Athena Phratria 18.Strategeion 19.House of Simon & Agora boundary stone 20.South Stoa I 21.Mint 22.Columned court 23.State prison (outside the map) 24.Temple of Aphrodite Ourania (location uncertain) 25.Stoa of Herms (location unknown)

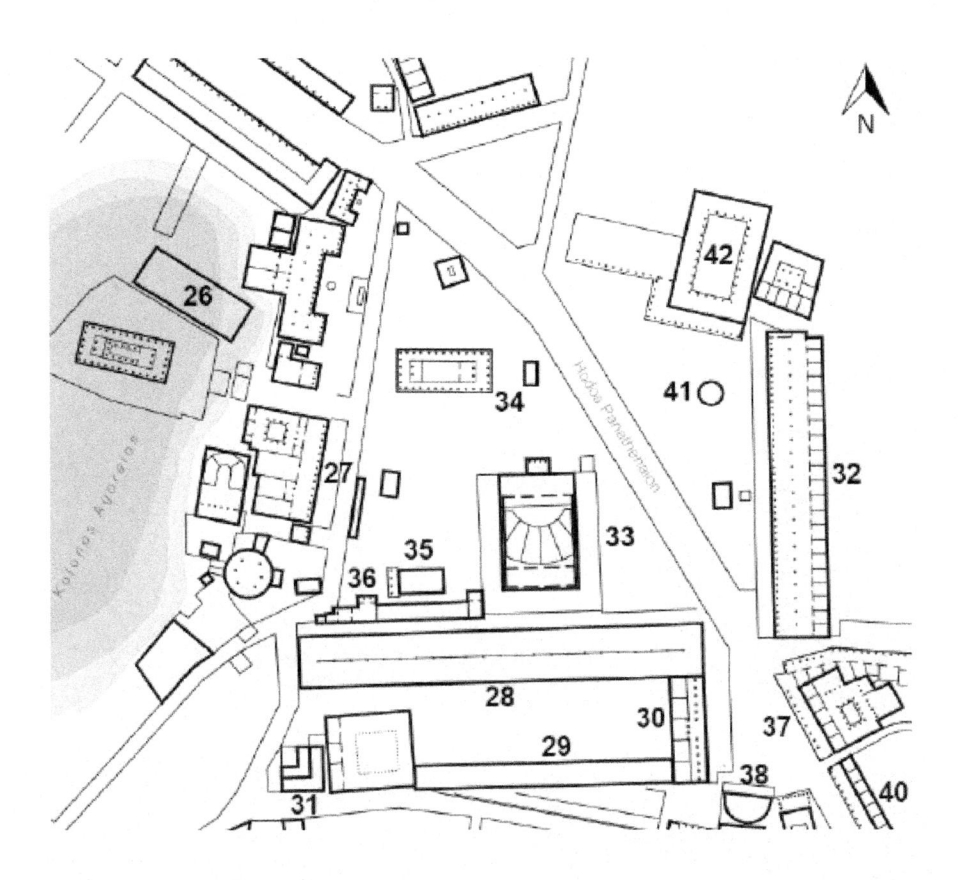

Plan of the Agora of Athens during the Roman period. Source: Tomisti, CC BY-SA 4.0 <https://creativecommons.org/licenses/by-sa/4.0>, via Wikimedia Commons

26.Arsenal 27.New Metroon 28.Middle Stoa 29.South Stoa II 30.East Building 31.Southwest Fountain House 32.Stoa of Attalos 33.Odeon of Agrippa 34.Temple and altar of Ares 35.Southwest Temple 36.Building of the officials 37.Library of Pantainos 38.Nymphaeum 39.Southeast Temple 40.Southeast Stoa 41.Monopteros 42.Basilica

Ancient Agora. The temple of Hephaistos, commonly known as Theseion. The upper photo was taken on a winter day when the mountains surrounding the Attica basin were covered by snow

The restored Stoa (portico) of Attalos, now housing the Museum of the Ancient Agora

The Agora was the heart of ancient Athens, the focus of political, commercial, administrative, and social activity, the religious and cultural centre, and the seat of justice.

The site was occupied without interruption in all periods of the city's history. It was used as a residential and burial area as early as the Late Neolithic period (3000 BC). Early in the 6th century BC, the Agora became a public area.

After a series of repairs and remodelling, it reached its final rectangular form in the 2nd century BC. Extensive building activity took place after the city's destruction by the Persians in 480 BC, by the Romans in 86 BC, and by the Heruli in 267 AD. After the Slavic invasion in 580 AD, it was gradually abandoned. From the Byzantine period until after 1834, when Athens became the capital of independent Greece, the Agora became a residential area.

In 1890-91, a deep trench cut for the Athens-Piraeus metropolitan railway brought to light the ruins of ancient buildings. In 1931 the American School of Classical Studies started systematic excavations. In order to uncover the whole area of the Agora around 400 modern buildings were demolished, which corresponded to the whole quarter of Vlasarou. You can see photos of it in the nearby metro station of Theseion.

The Agora is a flat area defined by the rock of the Acropolis and the hill of Areopagus to the South and the hill of Kolonos Agoraios to the West. It is traversed by one of the most important ancient roads, the Panathenaic Way, leading to the Acropolis from the main gate of the city, the Dipylon Gate, which we saw in the Kerameikos. This road served as the processional way for the great parade of the Panathenaic festival, which was held to honour the city patron goddess Athena.

To the North, near the middle of the open square, lay the Altar of the Twelve Gods (522/1 BC). The sanctuary was a place of asylum. The altar was also considered the heart of Athens, the central milestone from which distances to outside places were measured.

The most important public buildings and temples were built from the 6th to the 2nd century BC at the foot of the hill of Kolonos Agoraios, along one of the busiest roads of the Agora, conventionally called West Road.

The Tholos (470 BC), a circular building, served as the headquarters of the fifty prytaneis (officials) of the Boule (senate of 500). The New Bouleuterion was the meeting place of the Boule, the law-making body that drafted law bills for subsequent discussion and approval in the Assembly (Ecclesia), which, as we saw previously, gathered in the Pnyx. The Metroon (2nd century BC) served both as a sanctuary of the Mother of the Gods and the archive building of the city. The monument of the Eponymous Heroes (350 BC) was a long base for the ten bronze statues representing the heroes whose names were borne by the ten tribes of Athens. On the western side of the Agora there are also the remains of the Ionic temple of Apollo Patroos (Fatherly) (325 BC), so-called because he was the father of Ion, founder of the Ionian Greeks, a tribe that included the Athenians; also, the cella of the small temple of Zeus Phratrios and Athena Phratria (350 BC), who were the principal deities of the ancestral religious brotherhoods or phratries; moreover, the stoa (portico) of Zeus Eleutherios (of Freedom), whose cult was established after the battle of Plataea in 479 BC, when the Greeks drove the Persians out of Greece; and finally, the stoa Basileios (Royal stoa), the headquarters of the archon basileus, the official responsible for religious matters and the laws.

Overlooking the Agora from the hill to the West (Kolonos Agoraios) is the temple of Hephaistos and Athena (second half of 5th century BC), popularly known as 'Theseion', because, after ancient times, people confused it with the temple of Theseus.

In the northwest, excavations revealed the inscribed marble posts that were used to mark the entrances to the Agora wherever a street led into the open square. One of them with the inscription 'I am the boundary stone of the Agora' (500 BC) was found by the house of Simon the cobbler, where Socrates used to meet his pupils.

Further to the northwest starts the valley leading toward the Pnyx. Here are the complex remains of a residential and commercial area, the so-called 'Industrial District'. One larger structure, the 'Poros Building', has been tentatively identified as the Desmoterion (state prison) where Socrates was executed.

To the South, the Agora was lined by various public buildings: the Southwest Fountain House (340-325 BC), the Aiakeion -formerly identified as the Heliaia- (early 5th century BC), the South Stoa I (430-420 BC), the South Stoa II (2nd century BC), the Southeast Fountain House (530-520 BC) and the Mint (400 BC).

The church of the Holy Apostles, dating from around 1000 AD, was part of the Byzantine settlement.

The Middle Stoa, built in the 2nd century BC, served a primarily commercial function. It divided the old square into two unequal halves. In the northern half of the old Agora square in the years around 15 BC, a large concert hall (odeon) was offered to the Athenians by Marcus Vipsanius Agrippa. It was later adorned with a facade supported by pillars carved in the form of colossal giants and tritons. In the 19th century, four of these figures were restored.

North of the odeon lie the ruins of the Doric peripteral temple of Ares, brought in pieces from Pallene and rebuilt in the Agora during the Roman period.

On the northern side of the Agora across modern Hadrian Street, the excavations have revealed another large stoa identified as the Stoa Poikile (namely, the Painted Stoa, from the panel paintings that once adorned it).

The eastern side of the Agora is lined by the Stoa of Attalos, originally erected during the 2nd century BC as a gift of the king of Pergamon, Attalos II, to Athens. It was fully restored in the 1950s to serve as the Museum of the Agora. The museum holds archaeological finds coming from the systematic excavations of the American School of Classical Studies in the area and dateing from the Neolithic to the Post-byzantine and Ottoman periods.

If you exit the Agora and continue on Adrianou Street, you will reach Monastiraki Square. In this way, the end of this itinerary will meet the end of the first one through Plaka.

The whole program of interventions within the Project of the 'Great Promenade' is completed with the restoration of byzantine churches and neoclassical houses in the historical centre, as well as their connection to the rest of the city, through as many ancient streets as possible. It is the biggest intervention ever made in Athens since it became the capital of Greece and the realization of a dream of 170 years.

With the completion of the three itineraries, you will have complete knowledge of the whole history of this multi-layered city and of its main sights representing all the periods of its long journey through time.

The Ancient Agora with the Byzantine church of the Holy Apostles, dating from around 1000 AD

About the author

Denis Roubien holds a PhD in Architectural History and is a professor in Higher Education and fervent cultural hiker. The hiking trips in which he participates, along with other travel experiences, are recorded in his books.

Thank you for reading this book. If you have the time, a review would be very helpful.

Printed in Great Britain
by Amazon

Copyright © 2020 M Gordon

All rights reserved. No portion of this may be reproduced or stored in a retrieval system or transmitted in any form by any means—mechanical, electronic, photocopying, recording or otherwise—without the express written permission of the author, except for the use of brief quotations and reviews. The author has made every effort to ensure the accuracy of the information within this book was correct at the time of publication. The author does not assume and hereby disclaims any liability to any party for any loss, damage, or disruption caused by errors or omissions, whether such errors or omissions result from accident, negligence, or any other cause. Printed and bound in the United States.

M GORDON

How To Get Over A Crush: Getting Over Someone You've Never Dated

M GORDON